HANOVER COURTHOUSE.

HANOVER COUNTY

Its History and Legends

By ROSEWELL PAGE, D. Litt.

Salve, magna parens frugum, Saturnia tellus,
Magna virum; tibi res antiquae laudis et artis
Ingredior.   Virgil, Geo II, 173.

Reprinted by ·

HIGGINSON BOOK COMPANY
148 Washington Street, Post Office Box 778
Salem, Massachusetts 01970

Phone: 508*/745-7170   *Fax:* 508*/745-8025

*area code will be changed from 508/ to 978/ in May, 1998

A complete catalog of thousands of genealogy and local
history reprints is available from Higginson Books.
Please write or call to order, or for more information.

*This facsimile reprint has been photoreproduced on acid-
free paper. Hardcover bindings are Class A archival quality.*

Printed 1997

DEDICATION

To my Father, Mother and Brothers
and
To all others who loved or lived in
the County of Hanover

TABLE OF CONTENTS

INTRODUCTION

It is an ambitious task to write the history and record the legends of a great county and its people. If the name of any good citizen, or any noble deed, or good story has been rescued from oblivion, the task has been justified.

If the names and fame of persons and places here detailed shall not be deemed worthy to be studied and remembered, the author shall at least be entitled to the legend put by the nymphs over Phaeton when he failed in his efforts to drive the chariot of The Sun—"*Magnis tamen excidit ausis.*"

The language of another mythical character, mentioned by the same Latin poet, may be quoted who exclaimed, when a doubt was expressed as to the success of an undertaking— "*Sed, quid tentare nocebit*"—which question may well be deemed the standard of all adventure. Considering the fame that came to the Rev. Gilbert White, who wrote of the birds and beetles and other fauna of the small parish of Selborne, one feels that a true picture of the people, places and things of this typical midland county of Virginia may be well worth preserving.

Many dramatic scenes have been enacted within the confines of this county and it has furnished many notable *dramatis personae*. Here was born the greatest orator of his time and the equal, perhaps, of any orator of any time. From Hanover went the greatest party leader, whose ideas have dominated this country for a hundred years. Here died the most virile Virginian of the Revolution after Washington, and their names are the only two Americans mentioned on the monument of victory at Yorktown. As typical of the women the county furnished the wife of a great bishop and the wife of a great president. Here was fought by the greatest soldiers of the century, the bloodiest battle of recorded time for the hour that it lasted. Here lived one of the famous cavalry brigadiers, and three of the dozen famous colonels of artillery of the Army of Northern Virginia. Here was the home of the great sanitarian whose work ranks him with the great benefactors of the race. Here was born a writer who ranks with the best writers of his time and was afterwards known as a successful diplomat at a great foreign court during the trying time of the World War. From Hanover went forth two or more great foreign missionaries. Here have been great schools which have diffused the light of knowledge. One of them now in its bloom, has established beyond question the value of Plato's Academy, where teacher and scholar know, and are known to, each other. And here now dwells, as the result no doubt of such examples and such environment, a typically ideal American citizenship—confident, self-reliant and independent. All of which may be read in this book, whose author prays that it may be worthy of that which it attempts to portray.

PATRICK HENRY.

THE CHRISTENING

The County of Hanover, or the "Old County of Han-over" as it is affectionately called by those who are fortunate enough to have been born and lived within its borders, or to be the descendants of those born or who have lived there, was cut off from New Kent in 1720, as New Kent had been formed from York County in 1654. Charles River County was formed in 1634, and given the name of York in 1642. (Report Sec'y Commonwealth 1923.)

The History of Hanover, except as to individuals and local incidents, is practically the history of Middle Virginia. Within the century following the Yeardley Convention of 1619 at which were representatives of eleven plantations, the house of Hanover succeeded that of the Stuarts on the British throne, in spite of the efforts to restore the Stuarts. So the new county was named after the ruling House of Great Britain.

The population of the County in 1790 was 14,754; in 1860, 17,222; in 1920, 18,088. The county is marked on its eastern boundary by the Matadequin or Matdequin, or Matquin Creek which empties into the Pamunkey river, and by a line drawn from the Creek to the Chickahominy Swamp. Hanover is at present, and has been since Louisa was cut off in 1742, shaped like a bag of meal tied in the middle and swung diagonally to Richmond. There are three magisterial districts. Beaver Dam District is separated from Ashland District by the South Anna river as far down as the R. F. & P. Railroad; thence by the railroad to Little river, and by it to the North Anna. Ashland and Henry Districts are separated by the C. & O. Railway from the Chickahominy up to a point just east of Blanton's Crossing; thence by a line through the school house near St. Paul's Church; thence along the road to Littlepage's bridge at the North Anna. From the lower corner made by the angle of the Matadequin Creek and the Pamunkey river, to the upper corner where meet Goochland and Louisa is fifty miles, though the average width of the county is hardly more than fifteen miles.

The Chesapeake and Ohio Railway enters the county near the Meadow Bridges, famous during the Civil War, six miles from Richmond, and runs thirty-eight miles within the county, along its northern boundary. The Richmond, Fredericksburg and Potomac Railroad crosses the county by way of Ashland and Doswell in about a dozen miles. A trolley line connects Ashland and intervening points with Richmond. The line of the Richmond, Fredericksburg and Potomac Railroad divides the county nearly in half. It also divides Tidewater Virginia from Middle Virginia. The soil in the two ends of the county is very different. That of the eastern end is famous for vegetables and melons, while the western end is best adapted to the cereal crops and to "sun-cured" tobacco—the term applied to tobacco not cured by fire. During the Civil War cotton was raised, and is now being experimented with quite successfully.

The soil varies from pure sand to stiff red clay. In places it is poor and gravelly, especially upon the ridges in the upper part of the county. The low grounds however are generally fertile. In the lower parts of the county, the soil is underlaid in some places by green-sand marl. The bottom lands of the Newfound and Pamunkey rivers have long been famed for their fertility. And wherever there is a red clay subsoil, the land is susceptible of improvement.

FIRST CITIZENS

That part of the country now within the borders of the county was a favorite hunting ground for the Indians when the first English settlers came. No better evidence is needed than the arrow heads, spear heads and stone hatchets found in nearly all parts of the county. There still remains much small game, including some wild turkeys and a few pheasants.

The names of the rivers and creeks also testify to the presence of the Red-men, as do many of the common names of food, plants and animals, etc. The Pamunkey, Pamaunkee, Pamuneky, meaning "where we took a sweat," the Chickahominy meaning "Turkey Lick," are illustrations, as are the words, Pone, Hominy, Hickory, Persimmon, Chinquapin, Raccoon, Barbecue, and Moccasin. (Sams' "Conquest of Virginia," p. 323).

Stith says the Chickahominies were a stout, daring and free people. They took all opportunities of shaking off Powhatan's yoke, whom they hated as a tyrant. They made a treaty with Sir Thomas Dale in 1613 and called themselves Englishmen. He declares that "although Chickahominy is far from being famous for good land, yet they had the largest fields, and most plentiful crops of corn and the greatest abundance of all other provisions and necessaries of any people then in the country." This he attributes to the happy influence of Liberty.

"Orapaks," or "Orapax" was a hunting town and seat lying on the north side of the upper part of Chickahominy swamp, belonging to and much frequented by Powhatan on account of the abundance of game it afforded. It is described as situated "in the desert between Chick-a-ham-a-nia and Yough-ta-mund (Pamaunkey), that is some where in Hanover County. It was the town to which

Powhatan retired to be beyond the power of the English. Here he died in April, 1618.   The town was about twelve miles northeast of Richmond and consisted of thirty or forty houses.   (Sams' Conquest of Virginia p. 153).

Captain John Smith was captured December 16, 1607, near the present line between Hanover and New Kent. (Brown's Genesis of the U. S. Vol. 1, p. 187.)   It was this capture which introduced Pocahontas to become not only the most picturesque figure in American history, but to become the ancestress of the most charming of the Virginia families.   Once when a gentleman spoke of the uncertainty of the descent from the Indian girl, it was replied that the descent of the wife of the President of the United States—(Wilson)—was as well authenticated in a direct line from Pocahontas, as the speaker's was from his father.   Other Indian settlements in the land now embraced in Hanover were Pamun-co-noy on the Pamunkey river, Appocant on the Chickahominy, and At-tam-tuck about midway between the two rivers and near the New Kent line.   (Sams' Conquest of Virginia map p. 142).

Other Indian names of interest in Hanover are Mahixon or Mahickson, Tot-o-pot-o-moi, and Machumps.   Mahixon survives in the name of part of the tract of two thousand acres of land in the lower end of the county formerly Page's Ware-House, Hanovertown, of which another part was owned by the late Willoughby Newton and his sister, Mrs. Walter Christian, descendants of Mann Page of "Rosewell" in Gloucester County by whom it was devised (15 Hening's Statutes p. 278.)   Tot-o-pot-o-moi was the friendly "Mighty Tot-o-pot-o-moi" who with his men aided Colonel Edward Hill of Shirley when the small stream since called "Bloody Run" near Richmond ran red with blood in the fight with the fierce and war-like Richahecrean tribe of

Senecas from New York who had crossed the mountains and attacked the whites at the Falls (Richmond). It was this defeat of the whites and friendly Indians which started the wonderful career of Nathaniel Bacon the Rebel—the direct cause being the death of his overseer living on what is now known as "Bacon's Quarter Branch." (Mary Newton Stanard's Richmond p. 12). Tot-o-pot-o-moi finds a place in literature when Thomas Nelson Page, a native of the county describes the fine trees at Oakland as those "under which Tot-o-pot-o-moi children may have played." (Social life in Old Virginia p. 172). The name survives in the famous creek between Atlee and Hundley's Corner, whose historical significance is connected with both the Revolutionary and the Civil War, when Hanover citizens under Patrick Henry, and Samuel Meredith, marched across it from Merry Oaks to New Castle on the errand to recover the gunpowder taken from Williamsburg by order of Lord Dunmore; and when Jackson's army from the Valley crossed in the march against McClellan on June 26, 1862 on his way to Cold Harbor. It also figured in the Grant campaign of 1864.

Machumps Creek takes its name from the Indian whose sister was the young wife and great darling of Powhatan. Machumps went to England and on his return was shipwrecked on the Bermudas. While there he slew Namon-tack, son of Powhatan, in an altercation. This Namon-tack had been to England and was presented to King James I. (Stith's History of Virginia, p. 115). Machumps is shown to have been at Governor Dale's table. (Sams' Conquest of Virginia, p. 74). He is also quoted by Alexander Brown. (Genesis of the U. S. I p. 185.) It is thought that "Mechunk" creek in Louisa is named after

Machumps, brother-in-law of Powhatan.   So also with Mechum's river in Albemarle County.

Hanover County is bounded on the East by New Kent; on the South by Henrico and Goochland; on the West by Louisa; and on the North by Spotsylvania, Caroline, and King William Counties.   The line dividing the County and setting off Louisa in 1742 as a distinct County, was "a straight course to be run from the mouth of Little Rockey Creek on the river Northanna, South twenty degrees West until it intersects the line of Goochland County."   (Hening's Sts. 5 p. 208)

The act for dividing Hanover from New Kent was passed November 26th, 1720, having been enacted by the Lieutenant Governor, Council, and Burgesses, because of "many inconveniencys which attend the upper inhabitants of New Kent by reason of their great distance from the Courthouse, and other places usually appointed fc publick meetings."   It was enacted "that that part of the County which lyeth in the parish of St. Paul shall be called and known by the name of Hanover County."   The First Friday in every month was fixed for a Court in the New County to be constantly held by the Justices.   (Virginia Counties' Bulletin State Lib'y p. 200.)

THE WATER COURSES

The Northern boundary of Hanover is marked by the North Anna River which after its junction with the South Anna half way down the County, becomes the Pamunkey. Few Counties of middle Virginia are more conveniently watered than Hanover. In addition to the streams mentioned as being upon her borders, other streams flow through the county and add to the fertility of the soil and to the comfort of all therein.

The South Anna flows diagonally in an easterly direction through the upper end of the county, and bounds two of the Magisterial Districts until it reaches the Richmond, Fredericksburg and Potomac Railroad Bridge; thence it makes it way under the Chesapeake and Ohio Railway Bridge and joins the North Anna opposite "South Wales," and is known thereafter as the Pamunkey.

Little River and Newfound River flow eastwardly from Louisa in a parallel direction a few miles apart for about twenty miles and empty respectively into the North Anna at "Bear Island," and into the South Anna above Newman's Mill. Into the rivers named and flowing along the County's borders or through its domain empty a great number of fine streams known as creeks or swamps, the latter term being one of the earliest of the English names applied to the Water Courses of Eastern Virginia.

Within the Forks of the Pamunkey the streams of the county find their way through it into York river; as do other streams emptying into such Forks. A few streams along the southern border flow into the Chicka-

hominy, and so into the James river.   Some of the streams
of Hanover are Holland or Hollowing Creek which gave
the name to the old Colonial Church which formerly stood
in the Northwestern end of the County; Allen's creek which
gave the name to the old Colonial Church which stood in
the Southwestern end of the County, Hogan's creek, Pig
swamp, Bear swamp, Beaverdam creek, Lickinghole creek,
Jones' swamp, Taylor's creek, Rock creek, Cat-tail creek,
Tan Yard creek, Ben's swamp, Chis-well swamp, Turkey
creek, Mill creek, Beech creek, Needstone creek, Snead's
swamp, Rug swamp, Colley swamp, Fancy swamp, Cool-
water swamp, Hot-water swamp, Shop creek, Gold-mine
creek, Stone Horse creek, Stag creek, Horse-water
swamp, Mile Branch, Pug swamp, Bull Run or swamp,
Cedar creek which gave the name to the Quaker Meeting
House recently destroyed by fire, Falling creek, Beaver
creek and Gravelly Run, in the upper end.

In the lower end are Gunnell's swamp, Machumps
creek, Totopotomoi creek, the two last named after Indians
referred to in another chapter, Crump's creek, two Lickinghole creeks, Possum creek, Stoney Run, the Brandy
Branch, Powhite creek where Gaines Mill was which gave
the name to the battle of June 27th, 1862, a third Beaver-
Dam creek, on one of which Ellerson's Mill was, which
Mill gave the name to the battle of the day before, and
which stream ran red with blood on that fateful first day's
fight with McClellan in the memorable Seven Day's fight
around Richmond.   Other streams are Howard's creek,
Grassy creek, Boatswain's creek, Parsley's creek, Goodly
Hole creek, Black creek which gave the name to the
church near it, and the already mentioned Matadequin.
(As to the "mighty Indian King Totopotomoi, who was
slain in 1656 on the creek now bearing his name fighting

for the Christians," see Tyler's Quarterly Vol. 6, No. 3, p 216.) At the head-waters and along the banks of many of these streams are famous springs of soft clear water bursting out of the sand stone rock or bubbling out of the ground. In many cases these springs fixed the location of the dwelling. No sheik of the desert appreciated a spring of good water more than did the early settlers of Middle Virginia. The names attest the fact—"Spring-field," "Spring Grove," "Spring Garden," "Cool Spring," "Brock's Spring," and "Clay's Spring' are illustrations.

To recall some examples from other parts of the state: when Lord Delaware built the forts at Kicquotan (Hampton) it is related "that they stood on a pleasant plain having plenty of springs." When the act was passed in 1705 directing the building of the Capitol at the Middle Plantation (Williamsburg) one of the reasons expressed was that the place was plentifully stored with wholesome springs.

In April, 1737, Colonel Byrd advertised in the Virginia Gazette that a town called Richmond had been laid off with streets sixty-five feet wide—a pleasant and healthy situation and well supplied with springs of good water (Mary Newton Stanard's Richmond p. 21.)

In one of General Lee's letters to his daughter who had written of a visit to "Stratford" he says: "You did not mention the Spring, one of the objects of my earliest recollections."

A spring house was as much the part of the plantation in Hanover as was the dwelling house. Near it generally grew mint for mint-sauce, and mint-juleps then deemed innocuous, and lilies of the valley, about which Philip Pendleton Cooke the poet, and father of one of Hanover's best citizens the late Nathaniel B. Cooke, wrote. The spring path was ever the most beaten way on the planta-

tion and "having to be shown the spring-path" was ever
thought a saying to indicate feebleness of mind or body
To be long remembered by those who have heard it, was
the call: "Run boy, bring ole marster some fresh water!"
It is embalmed with the well remembered song of the
cradlers in the harvest field: "Water! Water! Cool Water!
Cool Spring Wat-e-r!"

THE MILLS

On many of the streams were mills which generally ground corn and were known as "Grist Mills." Some ground wheat and were known as "Flouring Mills." These mills were generally on the smaller rivers or streams and had over-shot wheels. There were mills on the South Anna and North Anna all along their route. Offley mill on Little River was owned by General Nelson's family, being attached to the residence of that name described by the Marquis de Chastellux in his Memoirs. It has been since owned by Ricks, Noland, Cooke, etc, and is still in operation two and a half miles from Hewlett on the C. & O. Road, and more than a mile from Coatesville on the Ridge Road. Rockett's Mill on Newfound river was built and owned by the Prices. It is now owned by Charles H. Oliver. Berkeley's Mill afterwards Scotchtown Mills, on the same stream was back of "Airwell" home of Fenton Noland. The Mill is no longer in existence, though evidence of it remains, and of the Mill road in the much blocked way by the Springfield gate running into Annefield back of Charles Cooke's bungalow, near Coatesville.

Fulcher's Mill on Little River was owned by William Fulcher, who lived at Goshen. It was owned by Thomas Nelson Page at the time of his death, and passed by his will to his family.

Rocky Mills on the South Anna river where afterwards Mr. Edmund Wickham lived and now owned by Frederick E. Nolting, was built by Colonel Syme whose mother, Sarah Winston Syme, married John Henry and was the mother of Patrick Henry. There were two Crew's Mills, one on the South Anna river and one on Taylor's Creek. That on the river is now Auburn Mills. Colonel

Dandridge's Mill was on the South Anna too. It was there that much of the grain for the army of the Revolution was ground. Howard's Mill is on the same stream. The Mill on Taylor's creek is known as "the Creek Mill."

Below Ground Squirrel Bridge on the South Anna were Crenshaw's Mill, two Morris Mills with Thornton's Mill on Mill Creek which emptied into the river between the two Morris Mills. Clough's Mill was on Cedar Creek. Blunt's Mill was on the South Anna near the present bridge of that name. Darracott's Mill became Ellett's and is now Newman's Mill. From this point Ashland now gets its water supply.

On the Chickahominy was Glazebrook and Thomas's Mill. It is on the road from Cedar Lane to Glen Allen. Gouldin's Mill is on Allen's Creek now called Mill Creek. High up on Taylor's Creek was the famous Mill of William Morris inherited by his son Richard Morris, and removed to Rock creek by his grandson Edward W. Morris. Now only the name of "Mill-field" marks the history of the noted plant. On the North Anna River were Anderson's Mill back of Beaverdam owned by the Terrell family Butler's Mill owned by Maddox and Dillard, which took prominence as one of the strategic points when in the spring of 1864 General Grant was trying to break through the upper end of the county to reach Richmond. Madison's Mill was just below Jericho. General Grant's headquarters were at Quarles' Mill, across the river.

On Little River besides these mentioned were Fleming's Mill, once Coleman's Mill, then Thompson's. Farther down below Fulchers and Offley already mentioned were Doswell's Mill at New Market where only the fine water power dashing over the pink granite is left. Snead's Mill once Winston's where the Hanover Academy boys used to haul seines, and Taylor's Mill near Taylorsville. Bumpass' Mill was on Stag Creek. Cross' Mill is west of Ashland, and Gilman's Mill is on the South Anna river.

In the lower end of the county were Oliver's Mill on a branch of Machumps creek, Smith's Mill, and Pollard's Mill on Crump's creek. Gardner's Mill, Haw's Mill and Talley and Gardner's Mill were on Totopotomoi creek. Parson Talley's Mill, Baker's Mill, D. Talley's Mill, Waddill's Mill and Johnston's Mill were on Matadequin creek in the order named. Now Flanagan's is the only mill on the creek. Another Baker's Mill was on Grassy creek just South of Winn's Church.

It is unfortunate that the names of the Mills should be changed as their owners changed. I find now no record of Shelton's Mill on the Pamunkey. Other Mills in the lower end of the county are the Brandy creek Mill, Parsley's Mill on Parsley's Creek. Ellerson's (Truehart's) Mill one of the two Bell Mills on Beaverdam Creek and Gaines Mills (once Macon's) on Powhite Creek, where the two dreadful battles were fought on June 26 and 27, 1862. Jones and Watts Mill stood a hundred years ago on a third Beaverdam Creek. Barker's Mill is near Grapevine Bridge over the Chickahominy.

Perhaps the most notable mill that ever stood in the county was one that no longer survives. Part of the dam remains, and Stoney run still flows whose water was impounded, when there used to come riding astride a bag of corn to "Lankfoot's" Mill on horse or mule the Hanover boy, who at the time of his death had become the first citizen of the United States. This mill was near the Slash-Cottage. The boy was Henry Clay, " Mill boy of the Slashes," and since his time or since he built beautiful Ashland near Lexington, Kentucky, the "Slash Cottage" has become Ashland in Hanover.

They who would see the stream and the remains of the Mill-dam, and even the post-oak tree to which Clay is said to have hitched his horse while waiting for "his turn," have only to visit Lankford Crossing at the East end of Ashland, and look about them.   Those incredulous as to the age of the tree may consult a forester, and if it is reported too young for a horse or mule to have been tied there a hundred and thirty five years ago, let them know that it is the scion of the Henry Clay Oak.   (See Map by Rev. Thomas S. Russell, Map by Boye, Map by Bishop Madison, "Hanover County.")

THE FLORA

The forests of Hanover have for years supplied an abundance of fine timber. All or nearly all of the hard woods of the Middle Atlantic seaboard are to be found in the county.

Oaks with the white oak and post oak at the head of the list, and ranging through the order usually classed as Red Oaks thrive there. Among the latter are the Spanish oak, black oak, turkey oak, pin oak, willow oak, water oak, chestnut oak, and possibly other varieties. Catalpas, locusts and cedar are used for posts. Hickories, Elms, Walnuts, Black Gums, Sweet Gums, Poplars,, the Ash, Chestnuts, Sycamore (or Planes), Lindens, Honey-locust, Persimmons, Beech, Birch, Hackberries, and the vile smelling but beautiful Ailanthus. In some parts of the county the pecan trees flourish and bear well. One of these is at the residence of the late Colonel Wingfield south of the Court House.

There is now little left of the "heart pine." This fine timber tree grew on the ridges extending from the Louisa line to a point below the Court House. It had matured slowly, and attained great proportions. In one case known, it was not possible to get the log to the mill with the usual appliances. The greatest material asset of the county is the short-leaf pine, which is indigenous to the soil, and will grow wherever a field is "turned out" and has the wind and the rain and the sunshine.

For many years the government has been experimenting at Oakland in the upper end of the county, in order to show the best method of growing this article of commerce and manufacture. In late years a new use has been found for this pine. It is being cut into "Excelsior" for packing purposes, and is manufactured into certain coarse grades of paper.   There is another pine known locally as spruce pine or jack pine.   In its early stages it is very unpromis-ing, though hardier than the short-leaf pine and producing seed cones earlier.   Its lower limbs grow down to the ground, though when thickly set these lower limbs drop off and after a certain age the wood may be used for poles or prop-timber.   It is usually too full of knots for plank or boards to be cut therefrom.   There is some long-leaf pine in the county, but not a great quantity of it.

The swamps and water-courses abound in willows and alder. These do not grow to be timber.   The sassafras grows spontaneously in pasture fields long neglected and in some corn fields badly cultivate.d   It is not prized as it was by the early English Settlers who loaded ships with it and sent it to England.   Other evergreens, besides the pines and cedars flourish in the county.   Among these are holly, laurel, running cedar, box-wood and mag-nolias when properly planted.

Fruit trees find themselves at home in all parts of the county.   The standard varieties of apples, pears, quinces, apricots, and of the small fruits do well here.   Wine-sap apples raised in upper Hanover a few years ago took a prize at the Buffalo Exposition.   Peach trees thrive only in certain protected sections, as the warm weather of March causes them to blossom, and the fruit is killed by the late April frosts. Cherries, currants, strawberries, raspberries, blackberries and huckleberries are at home and it has been shown that cranberries will thrive in our swamps and marshes.

The sol of the county representing as it does all va-rieties from red-clay to white sand is admirably adapted to the growing of flowers, shrubs, and vegetables.   The wild

A TOURNAMENT IN HANOVER.

flowers are numerous, rich, and beautiful. Water-lilies grow wherever water is impounded in low-lands, and every flower known to this part of the continent adds to the delight and wonder of the wayfarer, from the wee bluet of the early spring to the towering wild lettuce, of which the author discovered a new variety purple in color.

The glorious "Queen of the Meadow" which some botanists have called the "Joe Pie Weed" after an Indian medicine man, has a lavender colored globular head and adds to the lustre of any meadow in which it grows as it does luxuriantly in Hanover. Along any road-side are to be found wild-violets, pansies, oenothra, azalias and dogwood blossoms in the month of May. Daisies and dandelions blossom in the month of May. Daisies, dandelions, blackberry blossoms, thistles and milk weeds in the summer abound; while in autumn elderberries, pokeberries, James-town weed, yarrow, life-everlasting, the gentian golden and silver rod, the wild carrot known as "Queen's Lace," the many colored asters especially that charming little one called "Fare well Summer" make a show truly fascinating. Ferns, sumacs and the red berries of the holly, dog-wood, and spice-berry glow in the winter.

The hibiscus and scarlet sage grow radiantly in moist swampy places abandoned by the plowman or never within the sphere of his influence.

Perhaps the most pervasive of all the growths in Hanover is the broom sedge or broom-straw which the county has in common with the Middle Atlantic Seaboard. Epicures have said that the milk and butter made from cows grazing on broom-straw in the spring are the best in the world. This grass which colors the landscape with its tawny shade in the late autumn and winter, comes out

lush and green in the spring and offers good grazing to
sheep and cattle until the drying season of the late summer renders it too hard to be eaten.

The soil so rich in wild flowers produces the flowers
of the garden in great profusion and with rare beauty when
properly tended.   From the Rose-queen of the garden to
the tiny Alyssum, all are here at their best when well cared
for.   Nowhere else are to be found finer specimens of the
Tree Box than at "Hickory Hill."   Indeed the Box walk
there is one of the notable natural objects of the state.

Hanover is perhaps best known from an agricultural
standpoint as the home of famous melons and vegetables.
For generations, the streets of Richmond at certain sea-
sons have resounded with the cry of the cart drivers vend-
ing such melons and vegetables: "Millions! Mus'-Millions!
Water Millions fresh from Hanover!"   This cry made in
every key known to the music scale has issued from a ve-
hicle peculiar to the section, a two-wheel cart covered with
a sheet and known as "The Hanover Buggy." Packed
as these vehicles are up to the very top, they present the
appearance of a wagon train, as they wend their way from
truck patch to market, laden with the county's famous
products.

Ford cars and trucks may drive these picturesque vehicles off the roads; though the cart has the advantage
of being able to make its way over corn beds and stumpy
fields just taken into cultivation.

THE FAUNA

The Fauna of the County of Hanover is practically that of Middle Virginia. Deer are found here, and the good game laws of recent years have helped to bring back this picturesque part of the wild life of the section. Foxes, especially the gray fox are numerous and afford good sport to huntsmen, though wire fences have limited the pleasure of hunting, as it is now almost impossible to follow the dogs. The Ridge Road between Newfound and Little River is very suitable for enjoying "the cry" as Reynard prefers doubling back and forth rather than cross either stream. Of course this does not apply to the "Old Reds" of the "Green Scum Mash" who strike out for Caroline or Louisa or Goochland as the wind suits them.

There have been many fine "packs" in the County. Among them, Winston's, Redd's, Anderson's, Cardwell's, Blunt's, Cross', Mallory's, Morris's, Vaughan's, Lowry's, Smith's, Hancock's, Taylor's, Page's, Holloway's, and Wiltshire's have been or are distinguished. In many neighborhoods, "Piper" and "Cracker-jack," "Music" and "Rambler," "Rover" and "Crossland," "Trueboy" (who generally is known as "True-ball"), and "Silver," "Who'd-a-thought-it" and "White-Stockings" were and are as well known as their masters. The other day when "Young Kate" had a litter of ten thoroughbred fox hound puppies at Oakland, the naming of them was quite a function. It is related of Mr. Edmund Anderson that in buying a saddle-horse he was always particular to find out if the animal could swim, he being accustomed to put into the river wherever the fox and dogs crossed.

In Hanover, there is also good night hunting for those who like it, as there is no scarcity of raccoons and opossums.   Minks, skunks, muskrats, ground-hogs, and occasionally an otter, are captured and prized for their pelts. Flying squirrels and ground squirrels make a feature of the wild life.

The chief game of the county, however, are hares (improperly called rabbits), gray squirrels, and the Bob White (improperly called quail).   "Hares nest and rabbits burrow." "Yarrow Revisited"—Wordsworth.

The wild turkey is the choicest as it the wariest of all our wild game.   A few pheasants are found in the county, though the breed is diminishing so that it will require the aid of the Game Department for its reestablishment.   In the State Museum at Richmond there may be seen a white Bob-White taken in Hanover.

Besides the game birds mentioned, are to be found along the Water Courses wild ducks and wild geese, and in the season the wood duck.   Some sora are found in the marshes of the Pamunkey.   One September the author shot six sora on Jones Swamp.   Domestic fowls do well in Hanover, and the proximity to the Richmond markets makes the raising of chickens and eggs profitable. Nearly every variety of the song birds of our Eastern sea-board comes to Hanover in the spring, and many remain here during the summer and autumn. The birds that stay with us all the time are hawks, owls, crows and buzzards, field larks, doves, mocking birds, wood robins, kildeers, wood peckers, jays, cardinals, snow birds, and English sparrows.

In the early spring, come blue birds, robins, thrushes, wagtails, snipe, wood-cock, plover, cat-birds, cedar birds, lettuce birds, pee wits (called pee wees), king birds, (called martins) and other winged travellers from marsh-hens, storks and cranes to humming birds.   These include the bull bat, leatherwing bat and whip-poor-will whose iterant note is heard near any homestead on hot nights in the summer. Bees, wasps, hornets, yellow-jackets, and other stinging pests take their part in the life of the county. Good drainage has done much to drive the mosquitoes to the swamps and unreclaimed thickets. The spraying of fruit trees and vegetables has abated their pests to a great degree.

As much as seventy-five pounds of honey and honey comb was taken from a swarm of wild bees after years of effort. A part of the house was removed to recover this rich accumulation. This action may belong to the Chinese method of cooking roast pig as related by Charles Lamb.

There are few deadly snakes in Hanover. The copperhead and the spread head adder, known locally as the moccasin, being about the only two of that class. The black-snake is the most common. He is the friend of man in being the enemy of other snakes, and a destroyer of rats, mice, moles, and other pests. Snakes are enemies of birds and their nests. Terrapins, turtles, and frogs are found; and grass-hoppers, katydids, crickets, gnats, flies, and ants are part of the fauna, not to speak of other pests common to this section and climate.

The streams and ponds of the county have been frequently stocked with good fish from the Fish Departments of the State and Federal Government. The recent enforcement of the law for the construction of fish-ladders will help the propagation of fish in the upper reaches of our streams.

A small remnant of the native fish has always survived. Of these fish, the pike, catfish, perch, and chub are the hardiest. The introduction of the german carp has been

a great misfortune.   He belongs to the sucker family, and
lives upon the spawn of the other fish.   He roots the bottom of streams and drives away good fish who will not
abide such conditions.   The german carp is unfit for food
and no one, unless compelled, will eat it.   He is "a com-
pound of mud and needles" as Leslie Stephen says un-
justly of the pike.

Horses, mules, sheep, cattle, swine, goats, and other
domestic animals thrive in Hanover as well as in other parts
of middle Virginia.   For though the blue grass does not
grow here profitably, many of the teams of the county
compare favorably with those brought from Missouri or
Kentucky. Within the last year a Jack from the upper end
of Hanover took first prize at the State Fair.   The saw-
mill teams and the swift walking mules of the truckers'
carts already described are very fine.

That the county of Hanover produces fine animals was
long ago established by the famous stables of three generations of Doswell's at "Bull field" near Hanover Junction
(Doswell), from which went out that famous galaxy of
thorough-breds of which Nina, Planet, and Fanny Washington, King Bolt, Abdel-Kadir, Eolus, Algerine and Morello
were the most brilliant.   To Hanover, and to the stables
mentioned there trace back the most notable winners of
the season of 1924.   Not only My Own, Wise Counsellor,
Ladkin and Sarazen, but the great French horse Epinard,
who though crossing the ocean, and therefore perhaps running close behind the winners in the great races of 1924,
showed the "metal of his pastures" and the richness of his
pedigree as he had already showed it by leading everything
in France before he took the American trip.   (See W. J.
Carter's "Broad-Rock," News-Leader, November 22, 1924.)

THE ROADS

The shape of the county and its position relative to Richmond rendered the roads more extensive than in some counties of the same size. There are good maps, one made before railroads ran.

1   The greatest length of road is that which entering the county at Johnston's Mill on the Matadequin Creek, passed the Court House and the Fork Church and Anderson's Store (Birdie), and reached the Louisa line near the Brick House above the Gun-barrel road and not far from Locust Creek Post Office. This road in the upper end of the county is still known as the Court House Road, the Louisa Road or the Ridge Road. From the Gum tree where the Telegraph road crosses it just north of Newman's Mill on the South Anna there is hardly a stream that crosses it in which a horse may drink until the Louisa line is reached.

In his will written in December, 1788, General Nelson describes this road as leading from Anderson's old store to Yorktown. Below the Court House this road is known as the River Road because it runs in a general direction along the south side of the Pamunkey, and afforded easy access to Little-page's Bridge, Taylor's Ferry (Norment's Bridge), Hanovertown, Nelson's Ferry, Newcastle Ferry and Piping Tree Ferry.

2   North of this ridge road, ran another road from Louisa to Hanover Court House, following generally what afterwards became the Chesapeake & Ohio Railroad. The road came from Louisa near "Greenbay (the cross road just north of Tyler) and ran by Terrell's Tavern, Anderson's old tavern (Verdon), Taylor's store and mill (Taylorsville) to the Ridge Road at the Gum tree or at a point below;

thence by the South Anna Bridge at South Wales to the Court House.

3   Starting from the Louisa line at the Brick House already mentioned, the mountain road passed Goodman's Tavern, Higginson's Tavern (Montpelier), Shelburn's Tavern, Nuckol's Tavern, Ground Squirrel Bridge, Goodall's Tavern, and Mann's (Chiles Tavern) where it crossed the Chickahominy into Henrico County.

4   Another road from Louisa was and is the Crewsville road which enters Hanover just above Hopeful Church, and runs east—one fork leading to the mountain road above Ground Squirrel Bridge and continues along the Pounce's Track Road into Henrico.   Higher up from the Crewsville Road, a road leads south towards Goochland. one to the old mountain road, and the other to the old Three Chopped Road.   This last named road is shown on the old map as running about a thousand yards across a corner of Hanover from Louisa into Goochland.

5   Above the Court House, cross-roads run from those named as running length-ways, in nearly all directions. Goodall's Tavern on the mountain road, and the Court House appear as the centres to which the roads converge. In 1820 Ashland is not mentioned, but "Langfoot's Mill" is. The nearest points on the map to Ashland being Hendrick's Tavern, on the road from Goodalls to the Court House and Independence Church.   The Telegraph Road runs from the Chickahominy near Half Sink by Ashland and Doswell and leaves the county at Fox's Bridge, once called Taylor's, then Chesterfield, then Telegraph.   The longest cross county road in the upper end, was that which entered from Caroline at Anderson's Bridge, and passing Terrell's Tavern (Mantico) and Honeyman's Bridge over Little River, reaches Montpelier (Higginson's Tavern).   It

goes thence to the Crewsville road and so across it into Goochland.   The Gun Barrel road, and the Hell town road connect the Louisa road with the Mountain Road.

6   Below the Court House, the cross-roads are the stage road from Little-page's Bridge over the Pamunkey to Winston's Bridge over the Chickahominy.   This road passed Lipscombe Tavern at the Oaks, from which there is a short road to the Slash Church.   The road from the Slash Church to the lower end of the county is historic. There Jackson was to be on June 25 the night before the beginning of the Seven Day's fight in 1862; and it was the inability to make headway towards Cold Harbor that has caused military critics to wonder at the delay which is thought to have saved General McClellan's army.   Perhaps the most natural solution of it is found in the letter of Andrew R. Ellerson, a Hanover soldier in Thomas Nelson Page's Life of Lee.

Other cross-roads ran from Hanovertown on the Pamunkey by Haw's Tavern, Hazlegrove's, Dickerson's, Hart's to the Meadow Bridges on the Chickahominy.   From Haw's Tavern ran a cross road to Smith's Mill on Crump's Creek, and thence to Wingfield's where the road from the Court House across Machumps Creek, meets it.   The road from the Piping Tree Ferry crossed the New Kent Road from Johnston's Mill at Gardner's; thence by Old Church to Pole Green Church into the road from Smith's Mill across Beaverdam Creek towards the Chickahominy and Richmond.

Another road ran south from Old Church and crossed Matadequin Creek at D. Talley's Mill; thence by Cold Harbor crossing Powhite Swamp at Macon's Mill (Gaines) towards Richmond.   There are other cross-roads, but these give an idea of the way in which the county people travel-

led, before there were any railroads.   After railroads were
introduced the main travel of the county roads was to
them.   The great stores which made the fortunes of those
who kept them, passed out of existence after their introduction.   Anderson's store, Thompson's store, and Taylor's
store no longer exist, though David Anderson, Charles
Thompson and John Taylor made fortunes therein, as did
others in other parts of the county.   For the merchants
were then agents, factors, bankers and market men for the
planters and their estates.   Other merchants have arisen
in the county; but the movement to the cities, and the ease
with which the city is reached by automobiles have prevent-
ed the county merchant of today, having the same chance
for making a fortune that his fore-runners had a hundred
years ago.

It must not be thought that the highways described
were comparable with our modern system of good roads
with which the county of Hanover is so blessed.   Within
the last few years there has been great advance in the
building and maintenance of the roads of the county due
largely to the establishment of the highway system with its
centrally located offices in Richmond and with the whole
system of state highways ever before it for consideration.

The first piece of Macadam construction in the
county was that built twenty years ago from Beaver Dam
south to C. T. Terrell's Store (Emmett).   It was built by
the local road force financed by private contributions.
The Chesapeake and Ohio Railroad paid for one third of the
total cost which about paid for the hauling of the stone
from the Pyrites mines beyond Mineral in Louisa.   The
United States Government's Road Department lent the ma-
chinery and supplied the experts under whose supervision
a mile and a quarter of road was built after the road had
been relocated as to part of the distance.   Although the

material used proved to be not of the best quality, in spite of its having been tested by Government experts and reported on as the best material within reach, after twenty years of the hardest usage of any road of equal length in the upper end of the county, this road stands as the pioneer of rock road construction in this part of the state. A settlement of the accounts before a Commissioner of the county showed that the total expense of the road including the hauling of the rock, if it had been paid for, was about twenty-nine hundred dollars a mile.

Concrete roads have been lately constructed in the county which have given an assurance of permanent road building so far as any roads are permanent. For it must be remembered that there is no such thing as a permanent road, and that eternal vigilance is the price of good roads as much as it is of liberty.

One of these concrete roads reaches Ashland in an almost direct line from Solomon's Store in Henrico, and at Ashland divides into the northern and western route. Another runs from the Chickahominy to Mechanicsville and thence reaches Newcastle where there is a new bridge over the Pamunkey on the way to the Rappahannock at Tappahannock.

Good gravel roads run in long stretches. One from Ashland to the west, forks at Negrofoot reaching by one branch the mountain road near Montpelier, and by the other crossing the Ridge road at Pinhook (Coatesville) and going thence towards Caroline at Anderson's Bridge over the North Anna. Other good gravel roads maintained in the county run from Ashland to Littlepage's Bridge on the Pamunkey, and from Ashland along the Ridge road to Coatesville. Other gravel roads are found in the county; but they are for the most part maintained by local effort, rather than by "State aid."

THE OLD TAVERNS

The highways to and from Williamsburg, Yorktown and Richmond passing through Hanover required the establishment of public inns or taverns, termed in the law ordinaries.

When an ancient statute giving a list of such places as required a license, was cited, it is related that a modern judge condemned the punctuation of the public printer, and struck out the comma, thereby making the ordinary an adjective instead of a noun and declaring that the "ordinary" license was all that was required for Taverns, Inns and Hotels.

Many of these taverns were remote enough from the centres, to require a change of horses, and often the stopping of the yawfarer for the night. These taverns were after the pattern of the old English Inns described in the eighteenth century novels and were often kept by highly respected citizens of the county. Among the most famous taverns in Hanover was "Goodall's" on the Mountain Road twenty odd miles from Richmond, of which now remain but a hole in the ground where was the cellar, a great oak tree, an opening in the forest and a post office a mile away. Colonel Goodall was a man of much influence and estate. He represented the county for years in the General Assembly. He had commanded the sixteen men detached from the Hanover Company to demand payment for the powder removed by order of Governor Dunmore. On the same road some miles higher up were Nuckol's tavern, Shelburn's tavern, and Goodman's tavern. It was in the neighborhood of Shelburn's that the old minister of that name made the notable reply to the "ill-matched" couple who came riding up on the same horse to be married: "When a young man marries a young woman, it's all right; when an old man marries a young woman, it may be all right; but when an old woman wants to marry a young man, it is of the devil, and I will have nothing to do with it!"

In other parts of the county there were famous taverns; Terrell's Tavern, near Beaverdam and Taylor Tavern, at Taylorsville, and another one of that name on the Court-House road a mile or more below the Fork Church, just above Hanover Academy, Haw's Tavern, Lipscomb's, the Oaks Tavern and Chiles Tavern on the Hanover side of the Chickahominy where the mountain road crosses that stream. In old times one saw at these taverns some great man riding from south to north, or from north to south who would stop to rest himself and his horse, or himself and family, as they journeyed to and from the National Capital or the famous springs in the western part of Virginia. Many were the stories told of the great ones who stopped and how they acted,—what they said, what they ate, and how they looked.

It was at Taylorsville that Henry Clay spoke in 1840, and began his speech: "Friends and descendants of my friends!" The tradition of that speech has survived for nearly a hundred years. It must be remembered that the railroads have come within the century, which have seen the abolition of the stage coach and the country tavern, and substituted therefor the lunch counter, and the lodging room of the Commercial Traveller, in their turn about to yield to the camping outfit on wheels which includes food and lodging.

The most notable tavern in the county perhaps was that which stood and of which a part remains at Hanover Court House. It was kept at one time by the Sheltons into whose family Patrick Henry entered when he married their daughter, and gained the credit of being a "Tavern-Keeper." Mrs. Shelton was the daughter of Parks, the famous printer of Williamsburg.

It is of interest to note that when across the Tavern fence the young lawyer emerged from the Court House into fame as a great orator, after arguing in the "Parson's Cause," he had evidently lost no caste, for his father was the President of the court and his uncle was the Rector of the parish. His mother was the sister of that William Winston who Henry said was the greatest orator he had ever known.

COLONIAL HANOVER

On the 12th of November, 1720, New Kent County asked that their upper Parish of St. Paul be made a county. This was agreed to and on the 23rd, of December 1720 Governor Spottswood gave his assent to the bill. (Journal House of Burgesses 1720, p. 265). The first Hanover members of the House of Burgesses were Nicholas Merriwether and John Syme. These gentlemen and Mr. Thomas Randolph, member from Henrico, were appointed to carry the resolves for running the dividing line between the counties of Hanover and Henrico to the Governor and Council and desire their concurrence thereto.

The matter was duly disposed of by the County Surveyors and two persons appointed by the Court. A bill offered to have the clerk's and sheriff's fees reduced or abated was rejected, May 18, 1723.

On Tuesday the 24th of May, 1726, a bill was brought in to make that part of the parish of St. Paul in the County of Hanover which lieth in the neck between the north and south branches of the Pamunkey River and also that part of the parish which lieth above Stonehorse Creek, a distinct parish. This became a law on the 7th of June, 1726, when the Governor signed the bill. This was St. Martin's Parish. (Journal House of Burgesses 1726 p. 425).

After Merriwether and Syme followed as Burgesses Merriwether and Richard Harris; then Syme and Merriwether, and when Syme died Matthew Anderson. From 1734 to 1740 the burgesses were William Merriwether and Robert Harris. From 1742 to 1747 they were Robert Harris and John Chiswell; from 1748 to 1749 William Merriwether and John Chiswell; from 1752 to 1755 John Chiswell and Henry Robinson; from 1756 to 1758 a second

John Syme and Henry Robinson; from 1758 to 1764 Nathaniel West Dandridge and John Syme; in 1765
James Littlepage and John Syme; 1766 to 1768 Syme and
Samuel Meredith; and in 1769 William Macon, Jr., and Patrick Henry, Jr.   So in 1770, and 1771.   In 1772 Patrick
Henry, Jr., and John Smith; in 1774 and 1775 Patrick Henry, Jr., and John Syme.

The last entry of the House of Burgesses is "Monday the 6th, of May (16 Geo 111) 1776, several Members
met, but did neither proceed to business nor adjourne, as
a House of Burgesses.   Finis."

On the 29th of June, 1776, the Constitutional Convention that had adopted the Constitution for the Commonwealth elected Patrick Henry, Jr., of Hanover, the first Governor of the Commonwealth of Virginia.

On March 10th, 1752, the House of Burgesses rejected
the petition of John Henry, John Bickerton, John Merriwether, son of William Merriwether, gent, deceased and
Francis Jerdone, Executor of William Johnson, deceased.
That petition set out that there had been subscribed under
an act of 1740 money for building a bridge over Pamunkey
River from New Castle to the land of Edmund Littlepage in
King William County; that a contract was made with William Walker to build such a bridge for £ 130, which was
built, and a toll gate established; but that the gate was
soon afterwards broken down, and the people would not
suffer the same to be rebuilt, and to remain; that Walker
brought a suit against the petitioners and recovered £ 169,
7; 9; and 1644 pounds of tobacco which they have paid
The petitioner prayed for relief. (Journal House of Burgesses 1752 p. 28.)

Next day the Committee on privileges and elections
had before it the petition of Henry Robinson complaining

HENRY CLAY.

of an undue election and return of Mr. John Chiswell and Mr. John Syme to serve as Burgesses in this present General Assmbly for the County of Hanover.

After taking much testimony, it was shown that Mr. Chiswell had unduly tried to induce Mr. Morris, a Dissenter, to vote for him, and that in behalf of Mr. Syme one Higginson had given liquors to the free-holders, and that said Syme repaid him what he had disbursed for that purpose, etc. And so, it was resolved that Mr. John Chiswell and Mr. John Syme were not duly elected to serve as Burgesses for the county; and that the governor be addressed to order a new writ for the election of Burgesses, etc. (See 1752 Journal House of Burgesses, p. 62. The new writ resulted in the election of Henry Robinson and John Chiswell.

During the French and Indian Wars which were waged fiercely on this continent, the Reverend Samuel Davies by invitation again preached a sermon to the militia of Hanover at a general muster on the 8th of May, 1758, with the view of raising a company for Captain Samuel Meredith. His eloquence was most effective and greatly contributed to the arousing of the people. (Davies Sermons III. p. 68, Campbell's History of Va., p. 498.)

The Parson's Cause and Powder Episode.

The most notable meeting ever held in Hanover in Colonial times perhaps was that at which the people assembled to hear the trial of the "Parson's Cause" from which the young lawyer, Patrick Henry, emerged for his brilliant career as an orator of the first rank.

In 1758 a law was passed allowing all debts be paid in money or in tobacco at two pence a pound. As tobacco sold for six-pence a pound, suit was brought by the Rev. James Maury to recover his salary, which it was claimed had been abated by two-thirds. The action was against the Collector of Taxes for Hanover. The King by advice of the "Lords of Trade" declared the Two Penny Act void.   The County Court House of Hanover at its November, 1763, term decided that the law was with the plaintiff. At the December term the question was submitted to the jury upon a formal "writ of enquiry" which simply meant that the jury should determine what was the balance due Mr. Maury— being the difference between what was paid him originally, and what the value of tobacco was at the date the salary was payable. Mr. John Lewis retired from the case for the defendants as the Court had settled the question. The collectors then employed Patrick Henry, Jr.

It was the test case, and people came from all over the county and from the adjoining counties.   Twenty clergymen sat on the bench with the judges, the presiding officer being John Henry, father of the young counsel for the defense.   The Rev. Patrick Henry, uncle of the young lawyer, left the Court green, at the request of his nephew who said he might have to say harsh things about the clergy in the course of his argument.   The plaintiff's case was opened by Peter Lyons, afterwards president of the Court of Appeals, the leader of the Bar who relied on the facts above stated.   For the defense there was offered the receipt of Rev. James Maury for one hundred and forty pounds paid him by the collector Thomas Johnson, Jr.

Henry defended the act of 1758, and said that for the king to annul that act, annulled the original compact between the king and people, and from a father, the king degenerated into a tyrant.   The opposing counsel exclaimed that Henry had spoken treason.   Without noticing the interruption the young lawyer attacked the clergy asserting that from being shepherds they had become wolves, and were so rapacious that they would not hesitate to take away the last blanket from the lying-in woman. The clergy left their seats by the Court, as tears streamed down the face of Henry's father, and after five minutes discussion the jury brought in a verdict of one penny damages. (Wirt's Life of Henry, Campbell's History of Va., p. 515. "A Court Day in Colonial Virginia." —Prize essay by Anne Page.) Campbell, the historian, says "Henry's speech in the Parson's Cause, and the verdict of the jury, may be said in a certain sense to have been the commencement of the Revolution in Virginia; and Hanover, where dissent had appeared, was the starting point."

Hanover County led the way in appointing its Committee early in November, 1774, to carry out the suggestions of the Continental Congress of that year. The Committee took the name and assumed the function of "the Committee of Safety," to be "as Congress in its address to the people of America had advised "prepared for every contingency." The Militia of Hanover were notified to attend at Mr. Smith's Tavern (Merry Oaks) and there Mr. Henry addressed them, pointing out the necessity of a recourse to arms, and urging the formation of a volunteer company. This was before the battle of Lexington, and before the "Liberty or Death" speech in St. John's Church. (W. W. Henry's life of Patrick Henry Vol. No. II, p. 250). The next spring this same volunteer company marched to New Castle on the Pamunkey, and started on the march to Williamsburg to recover the twenty kegs of powder Lord Dunmore had had removed from the public magazine and for which his Receiver General was compelled to pay. Captain Henry addressed the Company and assured them "that the Hanover Volunteers would thus have an opportunity of striking the first blow in this colony in the great cause of American Liberty, and would cover themselves with never fading laurels."

Ensign Parke Goodall with sixteen men was sent to demand the sum of £ 330 as compensation for the powder which was promptly paid after the Hanover Volunteers had taken up their march to Williamsburg. The receipt was signed at Dorchester's Ordinary, New Kent, May 4th, 1775.

The effect of this action was felt in many sections of Virginia. The committee for Orange County met on May 9th, 1775, and passed resolutions "condemning Lord Dunmore's action and commending the seasonable and spirited proceedings of Captain Patrick Henry and the Gentlemen Independents of Hanover. The resolutions were drawn by James Madison." (W. W. Scott's History of Orange County p. 69.)

Governor Dunmore issued his proclamation "against a certain Patrick Henry of the County of Hanover and his deluded followers who have marched out of the county and put themselves in a posture of war."

HISTORICAL EVENTS

If, as already stated, the point on the Chickahominy where Captain John Smith was captured by the Indians be within the borders of the county, the Captain's adventure and the saving of his life by Pocahontas, daughter of Powhatan is part of its history.   We have already noted the incidents connected with the enlistment of troops for the French and Indian Wars, Davies' preaching to the troops and Patrick Henry's entrance into fame in the Parson's Cause.   Then came the recovery by the Hanover Gentlemen Independents, of the price of the powder removed from "the Powder-horn" at Williamsburg by order of Lord Dunmore.

Even before Hanover was cut off from New Kent the ancestors of many of our citizens had taken up lands, and made settlements thereon.   Evidence of great age and use is shown in the roads leading through the county from the direction of Yorktown and Williamsburg.

After the death of the "Courtly and refined" Lord Botetourt, William Nelson, President of the Council and acting Governor wrote that he had sent his Lordship's horses to graze in the upper end of Hanover.

Hanovertown at the head of navigation on the Pamunkey, and at one time called "Page's Warehouse" after the name of the owner of the estate, had once a considerable population, and exported annually as many as sixteen hundred hogsheads of tobacco.   When the capital was moved from Williamsburg to Richmond, Hanovertown was competitor and was defeated by a few votes. It was competition between the valley of the York and the Valley of the James. (Howe's History of Va. p. 293).

It was at Hanovertown where "no stone is left upon

another," that General Grant crossed on pontoon bridges
in the summer of 1864 when he tried to steal a march on
General Lee whom he thought he had left sick up at Verdon; but was to find, to his sorrow, across his path at
Cold Harbor where on the third of June there was fought
a second battle of that name so bloody to the Federal army
that the idea of "fighting it out on this line if it took all
summer"—had to be abandoned, and another line adopted
which took all winter and a part of the following spring.
Newcastle where there is a fine bridge over the Pamunkey on the road from Richmond to Tappahannock
was once a considerable village in which lots were bought
and sold. The Marquis de Chastellux in his "Travels,"
describes it as "the little capital of a small district containing 25 or 30 houses."

During the Revolutionary War the County of Hanover
was, as in the Civil War, "in the track of the armies."

The French Marquis just quoted writes: "the County
of Hanover had still reason to remember the passage of
the English "Mr. Tillman, our land-lord at Hanover Court
House, where we arrived before sunset, and alighted at a
tolerably handsome Inn, though he lamented his misfortune in having lodged and boarded Lord Cornwallis and his
retinue without his Lordship's having made the least re-
compense, could not help laughing at the fright which
the unexpected arrival of Tarleton spread among a considerable number of gentlemen who had come to hear the
news, and were assembled in the Court House. The English who came from Westover had passed the Chickahominy at Bottom's bridge and directed their march toward the South Anna which Lafayette had put between
them and himself." (Voyages de Chastellux II, p. 10.)

"While the main body of British troops was in Hanover County, and the Marquis de la Fayette lay between them and Fredericksburg, Earl Cornwallis had clear intelligence of the meeting of the Governor and General Assembly at Charlottesville under the protection of a guard in order to vote taxes, soldiers, etc. And so his Lordship sent Tarleton to "disturb" the General Assembly, capture Governor Jefferson, and destroy the stores at Old Albemarle Court House. The Marquis Cornwallis reports having found and destroyed near Hanover Court House ten French brass twenty pounders—spiking them and throwing five or six of them into the Pamunkey." (Tarleton's Campaigns p. 349.)

It is of interest to note that the correspondence between Cornwallis and Tarleton calls the "Three Chop Road," the "Three-notched Road."

The troops with Colonel Tarleton were one hundred and eighty dragoons supported by Captain Champagne of the 23rd Regiment, and seventy mounted Infantry. They left the army in the beginning of June, 1781, and proceeded between the North and South Anna. He had to stop in the middle of the day because of the heat. He pressed forward and stopped for rest at 11:00 o'clock at night near Louisa Court House, having taken the Ridge Road as already mentioned.

That the raid through Hanover made an impression on the community may be found in the fact that in the childhood of a notable citizen of the county born on the route of the Tarleton raid forty years after, his black mammy threatened him if he didn't go to sleep, with "Tarleton will git yo!"

It was of this raid that Jack Jouett, of Louisa, on June

4,1781, like another Paul Revere gave the notice which saved Governor Jefferson and the main body of the Legislature.   Of this raid, a Hanover man wrote:

> Tarleton the raider,
> Hell's own crusader,
> Tarleton, the terrible,
> Tarleton, unbearable,
> Rode as the whirlwind
> That wrecks all behind!
>
> A Hanover woman defied him,
> And the Church's Silver denied him
> As one who could not abide him:—
> A mad-dog, as onward he hied him!
> When Jouett in Louisa espied him,
> And enabled the State to deride him.

EARLY REAL ESTATE VALUES

The destruction of the Court Records of Hanover at the time of the Civil war was a great loss. These records were taken to Richmond for safe keeping, and were lost in the fire when Richmond was evacuated in the early days of April, 1865.

The records of the County in the Land Office, and in the possession of the Auditor's Office were saved, as were the two old Deed Books not sent to Richmond. These Deed Books arc now in the archives fire-proof building, as are the early Land books of the County. The Register of the Land Office has the Records of original grants—perhaps the most valuable land records which the state owns.

After the Revolution, lands were listed by Parishes, as they are now by Magisterial Districts. The largest land owner in the County at the close of the Revolution as shown by the Land Book of 1782, was General Thomas Nelson. He owned Bullfield (1278 acres) afterward the home of the Doswells near Hanover Junction, and Offley containing 11,698 acres. He also owned 680 acres in St. Paul's Parish. For the payment of debts incurred in behalf of the government, 8000 acres were conveyed to Robert Saunders, R. Andrews and D. Jameson as shown on a subsequent Land Book.

Nelson Berkeley owned 5695 acres; Thomas Anderson 1596 acres; George Brackenridge 1120 acres; Charles Crenshaw 1636 acres; William Dandridge 1316 acres; Peter Johnson 1140 acres; Hugh Nelson 1450 acres;Nathaniel Neison 1500 acres; Joseph Watson 1144 acres; Thomas Watkins 750 acres; James Winston 724 acres.

The largest landowner in St. Paul's Parish at that time was Charles Carter with 4165 acres; William Macon owned

2655 acres; Robert Page 2283 acres; John Austin 1753 acres; the Burnley's 2258 acres; William Anderson 318 acres; Nelson Anderson 499 acres; Richard Anderson 670 acres; Nathan Bowe 824 acres; Carter Braxton 100 acres; Joseph Cross 1360 acres; Holderly Dixon 1125 acres; the Ellises 821 acres; Richard Gilman 160 acres; Col. Thomas Jones 1020 acres; the Kerseys 330 acres; Edward Lankford 525 acres, Capt. Ambrose Lipscomb 543 acres; Peter Lyons 1650 acres; Capt. Elisha Meredith 252 acres; Benjamin Oliver 1072 acres; the Priddys 783 acres; Wm. Pollard 761 acres; Samuel Pearson 262 acres; John Parsley 150 acres; William Pate 300 acres; Mathew Pate 316 acres; Samuel Puryear 100 acres; the Raglands 1520 acres, Ann Sydnor 400 acres; Joseph Shelton 500 acres; Christopher Smith 714 acres; William Sims 140 acres; Daniel Truehart 2325 acres; John Tinsley 1085 acres; BenjaminTowler 1620 acres; John Timberlake 321 acres; Francis Timberlake 300 acres; David Talley 350 acres; Nathan Talley 225 acres; Joseph Thompson 677 acres; Burnet Timberlake 400 acres; Cornelius Tinsley 850 acres; Edmund Taylor from St. Martins, 580 acres; Geddis Winston 1250 acres; James Whitlock 433 acres; William Winston 250 acres; Barrett White 1081 acres; Berry Wade 250 acres; John Wingfield 668 acres; John Winn 900 acres; John Winn Jr. 600 acres; Peter Winn 400 acres; Richard Winn 370 acres; William O. Winston 910 acres; Robert White 190 acres; David Wade 100 acres.

The assessment of the Lands made by two commissioners and returned to the Clerk's Office where William Pollard, Jr.. was clerk is of much interest. In many cases the lands are still held in the original families. The commissioners (or assessors as they are called) were for St. Martin's Parish, David Anderson and George Clough; and for St. Paul's Parish, John Lawrence and Ambrose Lipscombe.

1782 St. Martin's	s.	L. s. d.
Capt. John Anderson's tract of 250 acres was put at	7.	0. 17. 6
John Ambler's 600 acres was put at	7	2. 2. 0
Henry Atkinson Jr., 100 acres was put at	4	0. 6. 0
Robert Anderson's (Cat Tale) 113 acres was put at	5	0. 5. 0
Robert Anderson's (G. M.) 405½ acres was put at	8	1. 12. 5
John Anderson (N. River) 150 acres was put at	5	0. 7. 6
Thomas Anderson 1370 acres was put at	6	4. 2. 2½
John Austin's (L. River) 100 acres was put at	6	0. 6. 0.
David Anderson Jr., 630 acres was put at	7	2. 4. 0.
James Anthony's 225 acres was put at	5	0. 11. 0.
John Anthony's (N. River) 474 acres was put at	4	0. 18. 0
John Alvin's 30 acres was put at	4	0. 1. 0.
Col. Rich. Anderson's 654 acres was put at	6	1. 19. 2.
Eliza Anderson's 100 acres was put at	5	0. 5. 0.
Martha Berryman's 507 acres was put at	5	1. 5. 0.
William Bartlett's 100 acres was put at	6	0. 6. 0.
Wm. Brown's 100 acres was put at	5	0. 5. 0.
Nelson Barkley's (Berkeley) 5695 acres was put at	10	28. 9. 6.
Dudley Brown's 241 acres was put at	7	0. 16. 10¼
Rev. Robt. Barrett's glebe 350 acres was put at	7	1. 4. 6.
Walter Chisholm's 250 acres was put at	6	0. 15. 0.
William Childress Jr's. 100 acres was put at	6	0. 6. 0.
Thomas Crenshaw's 470 acres was put at	7	1. 12. 10¾
Col. Wilson Miles Cary's 960 acres was put at	7	3. 7. 2.
Col. Nath'l West Dandridge's 700 acres was put at	8	2. 16. 0.
Colonel Charles Dabney's 350 acres was put at	8	1. 8. 0.
Home B. Dam's 805 acres was put at	7	2. 16. 4
George Dabney's 805 acres was put at	7	2. 16. 4.
Capt. Thomas Doswell's 769 acres was put at	10	3. 16 10¾
Eliza Fontain's 2100 acres was put at	7	7. 7. 0.
John Gooden's 415 acres was put at	9	1. 17. 4.
Joseph Goodman's 713 acres was put at	8	2. 17. 0¼
John Quaker Harris' 347 acres was put at	7	1. 4. 5.
Thomas Hewlet's 300 acres was put at	8	1. 4. 6.
Overton Harris' 1080 acres was put at	16	8. 12. 0.
John Hope's 289 acres was put at	6	0. 12. 2.

Benjamin Hancock's 150 acres was put at	5	0.	7.	6
Martin Hawkin's 2 acres was put at	6	0.	0.	1¼
Charles Higgason's 200 acres was put at	6	0.	12.	0
David Jones' 275 acres was put at	6	0.	16.	6
Major Christopher Jones' 664 acres was put at	6	1.	19.	10
Solomon Lowry's 150 acres was put at	5	0.	7.	6.
William Morris' 2600 acres (T. C.) was put at	8	10.	12.	0
Charles Mallory's 230 acres was put at	5	0.	11.	6
Nicholas Mills' 350 acres was put at	9	1.	11.	6
Maj. John Minor's 248 acres was put at	5	0.	12.	4¾
Thomas Nelson's 1278 acres was put at	20	12.	15.	7
Thomas Nelson's 11698 acres was put at	10	58.	9.	9½
Col. Sam Overton's 1428 acres was put at	20	14.	5.	7
William Overton's 1096 acres was put at	20	14.	5.	7.
Dr. John Powel's 840 acres was put at	7	2.	18.	0
Capt. John Price's 1059 acres was put at	7	3.	4.	11
John Phillips' 430 acres was put at	8	1.	14.	0
John Richardson's 1213 acres was put at	9	5.	9.	0
Jessey Rice's 120 acres was put at	8	0.	9.	7
William Stanley's 125 acres was put at	7	0.	8.	9
Dr. John Shore's 480 acres was put at	8	2.	3.	2½
Col. John Syme's 1400 acres was put at	8	5.	12.	0
John Stanley's 403 acres was put at	7	0.	8.	9
Robert Sydnor's 200 acres was put at	7	0.	14.	0
Capt. John Shelton's 685 acres was put at	8	2.	14.	9½
William Thompson's 397 acres was put at	7	1.	7.	9¼
Timothy Terrell's 252 acres was put at	10	1.	5.	2¼
Capt. John Thompson's 271 acres was put at	6	0.	16.	3
Maj. Thomas Travilion's 958 acres was put at	6	2.	17.	5½
Edmond Taylor's (at Lome) 380¼ acres was put at	6	1.	3.	4¼
Edmond Taylor's (in St. Paul) 580 acres was put at	4	1.	3.	2¼
Capt. Paul Thilmon's 600 acres was put at	10	3.	0.	0
Joseph Williamson's 169 acres was put at	5	0.	8.	5½
Josiah Woodson's 710 acres was put at	10	3.	11.	0
Capt. Isaac Winston's 1045 acres was put at	12	6.	5.	4
Thomas Wingfield's 326 acres was put at	7	1.	2.	9½
Capt. John Winston's 1440 acres was put at	10	0.	7.	4
Augustin Woolfolk's 572 acres was put at	6	1.	14.	3
Charles Yeamon's 286 acres was put at	8	0.	17.	1¾

1782 St. Paul's Parish:

Luke Anthony's 200 acres was put at	3	0.	6.	0
John Anderson's 100 acres was put at	4	0.	4.	0
Dr. William Anderson's 266 acres was put at	4	0.	10	7½
Joseph Bailey's 100 acres was put at	3	0.	3.	0
John Crenshaw's (B. How) 475 acres was put at	5	1.	3.	9
Joseph Clark's 60 acres was put at	3	0.	1.	9½
James Cawthorn's 153 acres was put at	4	0.	6.	1¼
Peter Christian's 100 acres was put at	5	0.	5.	0
Joseph Crenshaw's 750 acres was put at	8	3.	0.	0
John Davis' 268 acres was put at	5	0.	13.	4¾
Robert Ellett's 600 acres was put at	8	2.	8.	0
William Ford's 150 acres was put at	4	0.	6.	0
Major Parke Goodall's 645 acres was put at	7	2.	4.	10
Major Parke Goodall's (in the slashes) 482½ acres was put at	4	0.	19.	3
John Grubb's 100 acres was put at	4	0.	4.	0
John Hughes' 100 acres was put at	4	0.	4.	0
William Jones' 130 acres was put at	4	0.	5.	0
John Jones' 350 acres was put at	4	0.	14.	0
Robert Lee's 100 acres was put at	5	0.	5.	0
James Littlepage' 400 acres was put at	4	0.	16.	0
John Martin's 550 acres was put at	5	1.	7.	6
John Norvel's 431½ acres was put at	4	0.	17.	3
Samuel Puryear's 100 acres was put at	4	0.	4.	0
George Rowland's 156 acres was put at	5	0.	7.	0½
John Sneed's 434 acres was put at	5	0.	7.	6
Roy Stone's 190 acres was put at	4	0.	7.	7
Joseph Shelton's 500 acres was put at	17.6	0.	10.	0
John Sled's 250 acres was put at	4	0.	10.	0
Capt. John Stanley's 317 acres was put at	20.6	4.	17.	6
Charles Toler's 100 acres was put at	4	0.	4.	0
John Winn's 900 acres was put at	5	3.	1.	11
David Wade's 100 acres was put at	4	0.	5.	6

The Land Book for 1783 shows the following valuations, etc., for St. Paul's Parish:

Col. Richard Anderson's tract of 667 acres was put at	20.	11	9.	2.	8
Capt. Thomas Austin's 573 acres was put at	18.	3	7.	16.	11
Elizabeth Clay's 464 acres was put at	15.	6	5.	7.	11

Capt. Wm. Clopton's 163 acres was put at	9.	2	1. 2.	5
Charles Carter's 4165 acres was put at	18.	3	57. 0.	3
Ralph Crutchfield's 265 acres was put at	18.	3	3. 12.	7
Capt. Joseph Cross' 391 acres was put at	12.	6	0. 3.	7
William Darricott's 1000 acres was put at	20.	1	15. 1.	3.
Capt. George Dabney's (Slashes) 210 acres was put at	3.	8.	0. 11.	7
Wm. England's 209 acres was put at	7.	4	1. 3.	0
George Earnest's 661 acres was put at	11.	0	5. 9.	1
Thomas Garland's 796 acres was put at	29.	7	17. 13.	3
Samuel Gist's 2331 acres was put at	15.	8.	23. 19.	2
Col. Wm. Johnson's 218 acres was put at	11.	5	1. 17.	0
Nathaniel Nuckol's 126 acres was put at	18.	3	1. 14.	6
Capt. Wm. Macon's 2155 acres was put at	17.	6	25. 18.	0
Robert Page's (B. Neck) 2283 acres was put at 23.	8.		40. 10.	6
George Pickett's 795 acres was put at	11.	5	6. 16	2
Joseph Peace's 101 acres was put at	11.	5	0. 17.	4
Ann Sydnor's 400 acres was put at 0.	13.	8	0. 4.	2
Col. John Starke's 395 acres was put at 0.	12.	6	3. 7.	8
Col. John Starke's 235 acres was put at 0.	10.	0	1. 12.	4
Mtfflor John Starke's 337 acres was put at	17.	6	4. 0.	11
Capt. Thomas Richardson's 395 acres was put at	12.	6	3. 7.	8
Dr. John Shore's 273 acres was put at	9.	2	1. 17.	7
Col. John Symes' 1200 acres was put at	45.	6	40. 19.	0
Capt. Paul Thilman's 550 acres was put at	13.	8	5. 12.	9
Capt. Henry Timberlake's 369 acres was put at	18.	3	5. 1.	1
Capt. Henry Timberlake's 248 acres was put at	13.	8	2. 10.	11
William Talley's 100 acres was put at 0.	5.	6	0. 8.	3
Capt. Thomas Tinsley's 160 acres was put at	6.	0	0. 13.	3
Capt. Elisha White's 200 acres was put at	7.	4	0. 1.	2
Matthew Whitlock's 560 acres was put at 0.	11.	0	4. 12.	5
John Wingfield, Sr's. 668 acres was put at	13.	8	0. 6.	17
Wm. Winston's 550 acres was put at	27.	4	11. 5.	6
Wm. O. Winston's 360 acres was put at	9.	2	2. 9.	6
Robert White's 190 acres was put at	7.	4	1. 0.	11
William Wicker's 100 acres was put at	7.	4	0. 11.	0
James White's 300 acres was put at	8.	3	1. 17.	2
Cyrus Via's 100 acres was put at	7.	4	0. 11.	0
Littleberry Via's 113 acres was put at	7.	4	0. 12.	6

THE CHURCHES

The earliest churches in the county were those of the Established English Church. After the Revolution they had to bear the odium of the discredited English Government which combined church and state. The Rev. Patrick Henry was rector of St. Paul's Parish for forty years and the Rev. Robert Barrett of St. Martin's Parish for thirty-three years. The dis-establishment of the church was a fortunate thing for the people who belonged to it.

The earliest churches in the county were "Old Church," The Slash Church, The Fork Church, Winn's Church, Allen's Creek Church and Hollowing Creek Church. The two last named no longer exist though their positions are well known as described already in the Southwestern and Northwestern corners of the county. In place of Hollowing Creek Church, Trinity Church was built in 1830, and in place of Allen's Creek Church, the Church of Our Saviour at Montpelier was built in 1882. It was named after the church in Shanghai that had been ministered to by the Rev. Dr. Robert Nelson, a citizen of Hanover, who served there for thirty years as a missionary of the Episcopal Church. At a later period St. Paul's Church at the Courthouse and St. Martin's at Doswell, and St. James the Less at Ashland were built. In St Martin's Parish, the Communion service has the inscription: "For the use of the churches in Saint Martin's Parish in the counties of Hanover and Louisa 1759." The tradition is that this plate was presented to the parish by William Nelson, afterwards President of the King's Council and father of General Thomas Nelson, Jr.

Other traditions are that Mrs. Berkeley of "Airwell" with the sacred silver in a basket on her arm defied Tarleton at one time, and the county officials at another who demanded its surrender.   It is said that a pair of shears which she carried enabled her to preserve the cherished relics of a past age and hand them down for the benefit of the parish.   This silver is still kept in the same house by the descendants of the doughty lady—the Fenton Nolands.

Perhaps the most virile church-body ever in the county was that which bears the name of the Hanover Presbytery.   It was notable both as fighting the devil, and fighting the Established Church, with a zeal worthy of John Knox.   Samuel Davies, the great preacher afterwards President of Princeton College, preached with great effect in Hanover County, one famous sermon being that referred to herein, preached for the purpose of helping to raise a company for Captain Samuel Meredith at the time of the French and Indian War. (see W. W. Henry's Life of Patrick Henry). For the account of Samuel Davies and his life including his diary while in England see Foote's Sketches (1st Series, p. 228).   In 1754, he preached, near Cold Harbor, the funeral sermon of Mr. James Hooper on I Peter IV. 18, the text selected by Mr. Hooper.

On the 10th of July, 1755, General Braddock was defeated. When the news came Mr. Davies preached in Hanover, and urged the young men of Captain Overton's Company to "be of good courage and play the men, etc" quoting Second Samuel X-12.   It was in this sermon that he spoke of Washington: "I may point out to the public that heroic youth, Col. Washington, whom I cannot but hope Providence has hitherto preserved in so signal a manner, for some important service."

It is of interest to note that among the descendants of the great Presbyterian, Samuel Davies, was the late Bishop Francis M. Whittle of the Episcopal Church, who exhibited

RANDOLPH-MACON COLLEGE.

much of the eloquence and dogmatic piety of his great ancestor. (See Slaughter's History of Bristol Parish p 201, 203, 2nd. ed.) Davies yet has descendants in the county.

The Presbyterian Churches now in Hanover County are at Bethlehem, near New Castle, Salem, and Beulah, in the eastern part of the county. From one home near the battlefield of Mechanicsville nine Presbyterian ministers have gone forth—The Whites.

The Baptist Church has always been very strong in Hanover. The early records are filled with petitions demanding the right of the Baptists to worship God according to their own conscience. Justice has been done them in the writings of the period to show what they accomplished in the way of religious freedom. They have flourishing churches in all parts of the county from Hopeful, on the Louisa line, to the Black Creek Church near the New Kent border. Perhaps their strongest churches are the Hopeful, Ashland, Berea, Taylorsville, Elon, Mount Olivet, Walnut Grove and Cool Spring Churches. Winn' Church, established in 1776, on the graded road above the R., F. & P. Railroad, is the oldest Baptist Church in the County, and Black Creek Church, established in 1777, is the next. An interesting fact about the last named church is that it was organized by the Rev. John Clay, father of the great Henry Clay, who in his dying hours showed the confidence in Christ's sacrifice which consoled him so perfectly, as he himself declared. Other Baptist Churches in the County are New Bethesda, near Linney's corner on the road to Richmond.—The first Bethesda built in 1830 on the land of Edward G. Sydnor was destroyed by fire. The Trustees were Charles Talley, Edward G. Sydnor, John Jones, Miles H. Gardner, John Gibson, Bowling Starke, William Allen, Gibson Via, William Truehart,

Burwell Starke and Henry Curtis. The Gwathmey Church near the station of that name south of Ashland, and Duke's Chapel on the Ridge Road above the Fork Church are other Baptist churches.

The Methodist Church has always been popular since its foundation in Hanover, and a new impetus was given to it by the establishment of the Randolph-Macon College with its fine corps of professors, and its student body composed of all denominations but with the pick of the youth of Methodism. Outside of Ashland, perhaps the strongest Methodist Churches in the county are Shady Grove in the lower, and Shiloh in the upper neighborhood. Other well known churches are two St. Peter's Churches, Enon, Prospect (near Parsley's Store), Lebanon near Peakes, Little Bethel, Mount Hope, St. Luke's near Hewlett, Dunn's Chapel, the Beaverdam Methodist Church, and Rowzie's Chapel.

The Disciples, or Christian Church has a strong hold in the county. They have the old Colonial Church known as the Slash Church; then there are Gethsemene, Polegreen, Independence, Zion, Ashland, and Rockville Churches. Perhaps their strongest church is Independence Church, two miles north of Ashland.

The Roman Catholic church has its stronghold at Ashland where the family life of Mrs. Dr. Scott was a potent agency.

On eCdar Creek not far from Green Squirrel Bridge, the Friends or Quakers had a famous church, known as the Quaker Meeting House built about 1779 and which unfortunately was destroyed by fire a few years ago.

About it were settled a thrifty industrious body of people of whom the Crenshaws and Stanleys have descendants in Richmond and elsewhere.

There are a great number of colored churches in Hanover. Most of these congregations belong to the Baptist Church. They extend throughout the county from Bethany and Union Churches by Ebenezer and St. James by Chestnut Grove, St. Peters, St. James in Georgetown down to Shiloh, Mount Zion and Pleasant Grove in the lower end of the county.

The most notable colored preacher who ever came to the county was the Rev. John Jasper, who used to preach every summer at Union Church near Beaverdam to acres of people who flocked to hear this wonderfully eloquent old man who knew the Bible by heart, and preached with an earnestness never surpassed and with an authority rarely equaled.

A NEIGHBORHOOD CHURCH LIST

Since the day that the Caliph Omar destroyed the Alexandrian Library in which were supposed to be all the most precious documents and manuscripts of antiquity, fires have been the enemy of much valuable historical accumulation.

Our county has been no exception. The court records were moved to Richmond and destroyed when the city was burned at its evacuation in April, 1865. The destruction of private houses where church records were kept has made it almost impossible to give an accurate statement even of church membership at any given time in the past.

There have recently been found papers written nearly a hundred years ago which give the details of an interesting event, and the names and officers and families connected with one of the churches still used in the county.

On the 8th of October, 1830, the corner stone of Trinity Church, in the upper end of St. Martin's Parish, was laid by the Right Reverend Richard Channing Moore, D. D., Bishop of the Diocese of Virginia.

There were present the Rev. William F. Lee, Rector of Christ Church, and the Rev. Leonidas Polk, assistant minister of the Monumental Church, Richmond. (The last named became Bishop of Louisiana, and General in the Confederate army.) The Rector and the vestry of the Parish were the Rev. John Cooke and Dr. Carter Berkeley, Nelson Berkeley, Sr., Lewis Berkeley, Francis Nelson, Dudley Digges, Henry Robinson, James Byars, John Noel, Edmund Fountaine, William D. Harris, Jaqueline A. Berkeley, and Edmund Berkeley.

The church wardens were Dr. Carter Berkeley, and Henry Robinson. The building committee were Rev. John Cooke, Dr. Carter Berkeley, Francis Nelson, James Fontaine and Edmund Fontaine. The builders were William B. Green and Milton Green.

The Episcopal families reported as in the parish were those of Dr. Carter Berkeley, Nelson Berkeley, Lewis Berkeley, Edmund Berkeley, Jaqueline A. Berkeley, Capt. Thomas Price, Sr., Capt. Thomas Price, Jr. Henry Robinson, Thomas Garland, William F. Wickham, Philip D. Winston, John Darracott, William D. Taylor, Thomas Doswell, John Doswell, William B. Harris, Joan Noel, Euel Noel, James Byars, Pleasant Matthews, William Nelson Sr., Edmund Fontaine, Nelson Smith, Lavinia Smith, Nathan Thompson, Capt. William Kimbro, William Nelson, Jr., Abner Burnley, Dudley Digges, Richard Morris, Paul Doswell, Henley Doswell, Francis Page, Edmund Wickham, Francis Nelson, Hugh Pendleton, Frances Thompson, Sarah Thornton, John Taylor, Mrs. Carver, Ann Taylor, Mrs. Thompson, Mrs. Eliza Goodwin, and Mrs. Swift.

The churches in the Parish were: Fork Church, Allen's Creek Church and Hollowing Creek Church.

The Benevolent societies in the parish at that time were: The Fork Church Sunday School, Allen's Creek Sunday School, Domestic and Foreign Missionary Society, Education Society of Females, Bible Society, Temperance Society and the Meade Working Society of Ladies. The number of communicants were: Male 16; Female 49. The Right Reverend William Meade, of Frederick, was assistant Bishop. The last named married in the Parish and his second wife is buried in the county at the Fork Church.

EDUCATION

The private houses in the early settlement of the county had libraries of the best books.   The education of all the people was not then thought practicable or necessary.

In 1778 during the Revolutionary War the Washington-Henry Academy now a short distance from Atlee station on the Chesapeake and Ohio Railway was established by contributions made by the leading people of Virginia and named in honor of the two great Americans, George Washington and Patrick Henry.   For more than a hundred and twenty-five years it served the purpose of the founders, and has been recently utilized by being made into a modern High School with an agricultural feature. Thus the foundation established within a few miles of Henry's birthplace is still doing a fine work, and has been adapted to new conditions.

There was a famous school at "Meadow Farm" the residence of Mr. Wm. B. Sydnor, called "Meadow Farm Academy."   Here perhaps was raised the first Confederate flag in Virginia.   It was before Virginia seceded.   At Ellington north of Hanover Junction was, just prior to the Civil War, the well-known Fox School kept by the Rev. Thomas H. Fox.   Mr. Alfred Duke was a well known school master in his day.   Miss Haw and the Misses Campbell had fine schools and many families had private tutors.

Near Humanity Ford on Little River opposite a point two miles east of Hewlett on the Chesapeake and Ohio Railway, was "Humanity Hall," the school taught by the Rev. Peter Nelson, a Baptist minister.   It was at or near, the home of Captain Leland Butler, still owned by his son,

Austin Butler. At Edgewood, then the home of Dr. Carter Berkeley, was a famous Boys School to which, among other students, went in their youth Colonel William Nelson of Oakland, the Berkeleys of Airwell, and Judge William W. Crump, the distinguished lawyer of Richmond. Many years afterwards, Thomas Nelson Page attended a school at the same place taught by Charles L. C. Minor and his brother, Berkeley Minor.

"Taylor's Creek" the home at that time of Professor Charles Morris, was a notable school to which came and studied Judge Beverley T. Crump and his brother, Edward, Charles E. Bolling, and the late Judge Page Morris, of Minneapolis.

At "Mont Air," the home of the Nelsons, at the close of the Civil War was a fine school taught by Miss Jenny Nelson, who afterwards taught in Wellesley College and at Chatham. Among her scholars were the late Alfred Byrd, of New York, Nelson Noland and Frank Noland, Rear Admiral Hilary P. Jones, William Overton Winston, of Minneapolis, and Lewis D. Aylett, of Richmond. It was this same lady who built the first school house in Virginia for colored children and herself conducted a Sunday School for them. The good feeling which has ever existed be-between the races in that community may be attributed in a measure to this notable woman, and her work at the end of the war.

Miss Anne Rose Page paid for the teacher at "The School in the Woods" of which she wrote the charming book of that name. The Aaron Hall Free School was established by the will of that worthy citizen in the upper end of the county who left his estate to certain gentlemen and their successors as trustees "to establish a school for the children of his poor neighbors." This school except during the war has been actively run since 1844. Its endowment has been increased recently by donations and by the wills of Thomas Nelson Page and Marcellus T. Eddleton; and there has been added an additional teacher of Manual Training.

Pinecote was endowed by Thomas Nelson Page as the Florence L. Page Visiting Nurse Association.

In many of the neighborhoods there used to be schools taught by scholarly men and women before the efficient public school system was established. Miss Louisa Webb an English lady, was a notable illustration. For years she taught at "Beaverdam," home of the Fontaines. "Woodland," home of the Winstons, and "Hickory Hill," home of the Wickhams.

Within a mile of the old Fork Church on the Ridge Road in the angle of the Chesapeake and Ohio Railway, and the Richmond, Fredericksburg and Potomac Railroad, was Hanover Academy. This famous Boys' School was established by the late Colonel Lewis Minor Coleman, afterwards Professor of Latin in the University of Virginia, and was continued after the war by another distinguished artillery man, Colonel Hilary P. Jones. It is the son of this gentleman bearing his father's name who has recently been Vice Admiral of the Atlantic and Pacific squadrons of our Navy. Colonel Coleman's son died recently in Chattanooga, at the head of the Tennessee Bar. Many of those who have studied at Hanover Academy like the two just named, have carried its high standard of character and scholarship into all parts of the country. Of its memory, well may they say "Salve Magna Parens!"

Now, the most notable seat of learning in the county is Randolph-Macon College, named after John Randolph, of Roanoke, and Nathaniel Macon, of North Carolina. It was established in Mecklenburg County, and afterwards moved to its present site. Located in the beautiful grove at Ashland it fulfills Plato's idea as well as the object of its foundation. Under the fostering care of the great Methodist communion, its broad and liberal conduct has enabled it to attain to the heights of educational development. Learned and faithful men have ever had its welfare and conduct in charge—having in every way proved the value of the small college. There the student walks with the teacher in the grove as Aristotle did with Plato, and knows and is known by him. It is man meeting man, and not a mere cog in a machine meeting another cog whose only point of contact is that which in a regular or eccentric cycle recurs at intervals known as lecture time.

As a tree is known by its fruit, this college may well be judged by those whom it has sent forth with its degrees: David Taylor, the Rear Admiral; Tillett, the theologian; James M. Page, Dean, and Thomas Walker Page, Professor in the University of Virginia and Tariff Expert; Swanson the Senator; McLemore the Judge; Smithey, the professor and historian; Thomas Wheelwright, the industrialist; Walter Hines Page, the Ambassador; James W. Morris and Charles Sheffey the missionaries, and that list of others ncluding ministers of great power for good who are practicing the princples learned in this school.—all admirably justifying this great foundation, of which R. E. Blackwell and S. C. Hatcher are at the head of the operating forces.

THE PUBLIC SCHOOLS AND THE REVENUE

The Public Schools of the County are well conducted. To get an idea of their cost it is necessary to consider school population, and value of taxable property, and the amount collected as applicable to the schools; also the direct appropriations made for them by the General Assembly, as well as the amounts received from gifts and miscellaneous sources.

The population of Hanover as of June 30, 1924, was 18,088; and the school population 5,826, of which Beaverdam District had 1860 children; Ashland District had 1443 children; Town of Ashland District had 302 children; Henry District had 2,221 children.

There were in the spring of 1925, 130 teachers of which 89 were white teachers and 41 were colored teachers.

The lowest "grade work teacher" receives $55.00; The highest "grade work teacher" receives $85.00. And where the "grade work teacher" acts as principal $90.00.

The High School teachers and principals receive from $110 to $160 per month. Principals of schools usually receive a slightly larger salary than the other teachers. A slight bonus is allowed schools where a standard is attained of light, ventilation, etc.—applicable to all schools.

I. The SCHOOL RESOURCES of Hanover for the year 1924 amounted to $101,175.11. Of which Taxes collected were $43,875.41; (From Real Estate $25,998.76; From Personal Estate $7,775.90; From Public Service Corporations $8,185.05; From Banks $410.40; From Merchants $631.22; 5% Penalty $874.10.) TEMPORARY LOANS $5,845.98. Funds from State Treasury $48,346.29; (Appropriation for School Funds $48,316.29; Libraries for

Schools $30.00.) MISCELLANEOUS $3,072.36; (Donations $2,039.47; Tuition and T. B. Association $644.06; Scholars from outside $390.83;) Other sources $35.07.

For convenience, the total revenue of the county will be here considered.

The other items besides the above $101,175.11 for school resources which went into the County Treasurer's hands were: For general purposes $30,653.38; For Roads and Bridges $48,689.76. The TOTAL RESOURCES of Hanover from public revenue for the year 1924—(July 1st.) including the $101,175.11 of school money amounted to $180,518.25; Total balance for year 1923 (July 1) of all funds with the Treasurer $57,220.19; Total balance and receipts $237,738.44.

II. The TOTAL DISBURSEMENTS of School Revenue for the year 1924 (July 1) amounted to (1) $98,-318.52 (From County and District Funds $51,164.23; From State Funds $47,154.29.) The other Disbursements besides the $98,318.52 for schools disbursements, were for Roads and Bridges (2) $51,741.76; (From County Road Funds $16,101.89; From District Road Funds $29,518.39; From Joint State and County Road Fund $6,121.48.) For General County purposes (3) $23,649.15 (including $10,-940.99 for repairs of Court House, Clerk's Office, Jail, Jury, service and other miscellaneous charges.) For Delinquents and insolvents (4) $2,452.15. For Treasurer's commissions (5) $5,569.86; (on all funds other than school funds $3,173.82; on all school funds $2,396.04.) The above five items make the Total Disbursements of all the Revenue coming into the hands of the County Treasurer for all the purposes named $181,731.44.

III. Taking the TOTAL BALANCE AND RECEIPTS above mentioned $237,738.44 and deducting Total Disbursements $181,731.44 left in the hands of the Treasurer July 1, 1924, $56,007.00. It may be of interest to note that in the above Total For General County Purposes amounting to $23,649.15, there were the following items: Judge's salary $463.96; Clerk's salary $950.00; Commonwealth Attorney's salary $800.00; 3 Commissioners of Revenue, $2,816.14; Sheriff, $800.00; Board of Supervisors, $987.20; Public Health and Vital Statistics $207.60; Overseers and Support of the Poor $1140.85; Election Expenses $357.30; Police $900.00; Office Equipment and Supplies $800.00; Agriculture $1240.00; Stock killed (Dog Tax) $1245.11; Repairs etc, etc , etc. $10,940.99. Total $23,649.15.

The per capita expenses of the County to each citizen are $10.05, of which General Purposes have $1.31; Roads and Bridges have $2.86; Schools have $5.44; Delinquents and Insolvents have $0.13; Treasurer's Commissions have $0.31.

The Taxable values of Hanover assessed for 1924 are $8,218,924.74. (Real Estate, Tracts and Buildings (298,-511 acres) $3,845.825; Town Lots and Buildings $513,420. Personal Property; Tangible $1,333,375, Intangible $1,848,-022. Public Service Corporations $541,957.74. Banks, Capital $105,034. Merchants Capital $31,291.)

Hanover: County Levy Rate Per $100, 1924.

Ashland District; County Levy 25c, County Roads 25c, County Schools 0, Other County Levy 10c, District Roads 40c, District Schools 60c—total $1.60. **Town of Ashland;** County Levy 25c, County Roads 0, County Schools 0, Other County Levy 10c, District Roads 0, District Schools 0—total 35c. **Beaverdam District;** County Levy 25c, County Roads 25c, County Schools 0, Other County Levy 10c, District Roads 30c, District Schools 65c

—total $1.55. **Henry District;** County Levy 25c, County Roads 25c, County Schools 0, Other County Levy 10c, District Roads 35c, District Schools 75c—total $1.70.

State Tax: Rate Per $100, 1924.

On Real Estate and tangible personal property; Schools 14c, Roads 10c, Tubercular 1c. Total $0.25.

State Tax And County Levy Per $100.

Money; State 20c, County Levy none—total 20c. Bonds; (County, Cities and towns of Virginia). State 35c, County Levy none—total 35c. Bonds, notes and other evidences of debt; State 35c, County Levy 20c—total 55c. Shares of Stock; State 80c, County Levy 20c—total $1.00. Capital; State 85c, County Levy 20c—total $1.05. Bank Stock; State 25c, County Levy not over 85c, paid by bank. Income; (1% to $3,000, 2% on excess) no levy. Capitation Tax; State $1.50, County Levy none—total $1.50.

It is of interest to note that Public Service Corporations pay on their gross earnings $1.68 on the hundred, through the Auditor of Public Accounts.

By the segregation act, all taxable real estate, and all taxable tangible personal property, and the tangible personal property of public service corporations (except rolling stock of corporations operating steam railroads) and also the capital of merchants are made subject to local taxation only. Other subjects of taxation are for State taxes only. This applies to the year 1927 and the following years.

HANOVER'S MILITARY HISTORY

Reference has been made to the French and Indian wars, and the part played by citizens of Hanover, in time of the friendly Totopotomoi, when Hanover was a part of New Kent. Hanover's part in the Revolutionary war, like that in the Civil War, was considerably more than Counties in some remote section, because of its having been the camping ground of both British and American forces.

Of the 45,000 men in the military (militia) service available for the field from Virginia in 1776, Hanover had 900. About one-fourth saw real service. Those in Tidewater were subject to frequent calls, and the number from Virginia was very large in proportion to white male population.

In the Continental line, there were fifteen regiments, or battalions from Virginia, not including Continental troops from Virginia in other organizations and not counting those serving in the State line. In 1781 when Virginia was seriously threatened, practically all of the availing militia was summoned to the field. It is probable that about 6500 or 7000 Militia bore arms in the various campaigns, and of the crucial year. At that time "The State Line" was of some size.

Heitman gives Massachusetts 87,907 and Virginia 56,-678 altogether. These estimates are unreliable. (Eckenrode 8th annual Report State Library).

The companies listed as from Hanover in McAllisters "Virginia Militia in the Revolutionary War" are: Captain John Winston's company; Captain Thomas Nelson's Troop of 100 Cavalrymen, of which George Nicholas was 1st Lieutenant and Hugh Nelson, 2nd. Lieutenant. This troop well disciplined, marched to Philadelphia where they received the thanks of Congress and were discharged August 8th, 1778; Captain John Price's Company, which was in the South when Gates was defeated; Captain Thomas Doswell's Company, which was at Sandy Point in 1780; Captain John Harris's Compauy, of which Ralph Thomas was 1st Lieutenant, Thomas Jones, 2nd Lieutenant, and William Jarman, ensign; Captain Edward Bullock's Company; Captain Nicholas Hammer's Company. The last two joined Lafayette in 1781, as did Captain Frank Coleman's Company and Captain John Thompson's Company. McAllister mentions Captain Robert Bolling's Company as from Hanover; yet this was made up of men largly from south of the James—(J. T. McAllister's Virginia Militia in RevolutionaryWar, Page 7 etc.)

In the two years following the close of the Revolution, the following owners of land in Hanover are mentioned as having military titles. This was before steamboats, and railroads and the Governor's staff added titles in time of peace and though some of these titles may have been "by brevet," most of them were gained as soldiers in the Continentals, in the Virginia line, or in the Virginia Militia. Some of these land owners may have lived elsewhere, though the list is taken from the land books in 1782 and 1783.

Captains—John Anderson, Edward Bullock, William Coles, George Dabney, Owen Dabney, James Doswell, John Lawrence, John Price, Thomas Price, John Shelton, John Thompson, William Thompson, Paul Thilman, Joseph Cross, William Anderson, Thomas Austin, Thomas Richardson, William Macon, Joseph Gathright, Elisha White, Thomas Tinsley, William Clopton, Elisha Meredith, John Stanley, Henry Timberlake, Isaac Winston, John Winston,

Majors, Christopher James, John Minor, Thomas Travilion, Park Goodall, John Starke, Nelson Anderson.

Colonels—Richard Anderson, William Miles Cary, William N. Dandridge, William Dandridge, Charles Dabney, Hugh Nelson, Samuel Overton, John Syme, Nelson Anderson, John Starke, William Johnson.

Among the Hanover soldiers whose names are recorded among the petitions, or on the rolls of the Auditor of Public Accounts, or on those of the Secretary of War, that have been published and are in addition to those named above are: Barrett Anderson, David Anderson, Jr., Captain Richard Anderson, Captain William Anderson, William Anderson, Jr., Walter Austin, Joseph Bailess, Joseph Bailey, Lieutenant Bingham, Zachariah Bowles, Thomas Bowles, Joseph Brand, Edward Bullock, Samuel Bumpass, Christopher Butler, Dr. Thomas Carter, William Cawthorn, William Clark, Thomas Clark, Zachariah Clark, Thomas B. W. Coleman, Charles Copeland, John Crenshaw, Henry Cross, Joseph Cross, Jr., Fortunatus Crutchfield, Fortune Crutchfield, Thomas Compton, Robert Dabney, N. W. Dandridge, John Davis, Nath. Davis, Tolaver Davis, Tolaver Davis, Jr., John Davis, Jr., Thomas Dickason, William Dickerson, Henry Dickerson, Vicarious Dickerson, James Durham, James England, William England, Obediah Fawcett, William Gentry, John Gilman, John Gottlip, Hensley Grubbs, Anthony Haden, Griffith Haines, Norment Harvey, James Howard, John Hanes, John Johnson, Thomas Southard, William Tinsley, William Whipple.

Among the notable Hanover citizens with meritorious records was John Kilby, who served in the United States Navy and was with John Paul Jones on the Bon Homme Richard. For many years the name of Kilby station on the R. F. & P. railroad perpetuated the name of

GENERAL WILLIAMS CARTER WICKHAM

this famous citizen of Hanover. For more or less good cause, the name "Elmont" has been substituted, though as one takes or leaves the train at that point he looks in vain for "the Mountain" that was important enough to take the name from Hanover's Revolutionary hero, John Kilby.

THE WAR OF 1812

Hanover had its share in the war of 1812. The 74th Regiment of Virginia Militia was as follows: Captain Nathaniel Bowe; Privates: James Christian, Jacob Christian, Francis Taylor,—Alvis, Henry Arnall, Davis Arnall, Richard Arnall, Thomas Bowles, Peter Bowles, Ambrose Brooks, John Bell, Daniel Caker, Chas. Childress, Alex Chisholm, Cris Cawthon, Geo. Davis, John Donnelly, Pleasant Ford, Thos. F. Green, James Higgason, Norman Harvey, Ben Harris, Ben Jenkins, John Jude, Ed Maynard, Joseph Patterson, William Pearson, James B. Parker, Neal D. McCook, Thomas Richardson, Fendall Ragland, Thomas Turner, Joseph Shelton.

In the same (74th) Regiment, commanded by Colonel William Truehart, was Captain Bentley Brown, Lieutenant Wm. Smith, Ensign Wm. Woolfolk, Sergeants Thomas Taylor, James Sharp, Benjamin Spicer, Dabney Dickinson, and Privates William Arnall, Genet Anderson, John Butler, John Byars, Miller Brown, Nelson Brooks, George Bumpass, Thos. W. Claybrook, Richard Chase, John Dickinson, Lewis Day, Nathaniel Dickinson, Wm. D. Goodwin, John Gunnel, James Hall, James Harris, Terry Hewlett, Wm. Hargrave, Francis V. Howlet, John Hancock, Henry J. Hall, Aaron Hall, Zephaniah Hall, Jacob Holloway, Simeon Hall, James Hall, Tarlton Hancock, David Hanes, Garland Hall, Pleasant Hinchey, John Hall, William Harper, Benjamin Hancock, Wm. Hall, Wm. Johnson, Richard F. Jones, John Lester, Garrett Lowry, Wm. Luck, William Lawrence, Robert Mallory, Warner W. Minor, John Martin, John Moody, Nicholas Mills, Charles Mills, Thomas Nelson, Wm. Noel, Thos. Nelson (son of William) Samuel Oldham, William Phillips, Lewis Phillips, Austin Pate, Edward Patter-

son, James Quarles, Wm. Seay, Luke A. Seay, James
Smith, Solomon Stanley, John Stanley, Benjamin Stanley,
Charles Swift, Robert Sharp, William Swift, Strangeman
Stanley, Wm. Stanley, (son of O.) Wm. Stanley, (son of J.)
Thomas Stanley, Wm. B. Syms, Lewis Smith, Zachariah
Smith, Maddox Stanley, John T. Smith, Edward Thacker,
Chesley Thacker, Thomas Price, James Taylor, Charles
Terrell, Edmund Terrell, John Terrell, Garland Thompson,
David Terrell, Francis Thompson, Roger Thompson, Over-
ton Watkins, Thomas Watkins, Horatio G. Winston, Wm.
Wash, Richard White, Joel Walton, Pleasant Yeamans,
Austin Yeamans, Charles Yeamans, Preston Yeamans.

In the same 74th Regiment, Captain William Hund-
ley's company, under Lt. Colonel Trueheart, were the fol-
lowing soldiers in 1813: Captain Wm. Hundley; Lieutenant
John D. Hendrick; Ensign Nathaniel Cross; Sergeants
John King, John England, John Frazer; Drummer, Robert
B. Bowles, Fifer, Bowler Whipple; Privates William An-
drew, Geo. W. Adams, Thomas Adams, Thomas Bowles,
(P.) Thomas Bowles (F.) Wm. Bowles, John Bumpass,
John Bowles, Thos. Bowles (son of Ben) John Brock, Jo-
seph Bowles, Henry Cross, (son of John) Wm. Cameron,
John Cross Jr., Jas. Christian, James Donnally, Wyatt
Davis, John Donnally, Thos. Davis, James Davis, Jr., David
Edwards, John Glazebrook, Andrew Grubbs, Richard
Glazebrook, Richard P. Green, Joel Hanes, James Hooper,
Moses Harris, Fleming Harris, Garland Harris, Benjamin
Jenkins, Wm. Jenkins, Thomas King, Wm. King, Benjamin
Langford, James Lynn, Sterling Langford, Wm. N. Powell,
James Parseley, John Perkins, Samuel Priddy, John Prid-
dy, Samuel Patterson, Fendall Ragland, John Starke, John
Sims, Philip Sheppard, John A. Smith, John Stone, Benja-
min Snead, Wyatt Tinsley, Wm. Toler, Parke Tinsley, Wal-

ter Tucker, Henry R. Winston,   Jesse Winn, John S. West,
Christopher Winfield, Palmer Whipple.

The 74th Regiment, Colonel Wm. Truehart had   Captain Thos. Jones company, with   the   following: Captain
Thos. Jones; Lieutenant David R. Jones; Ensign Charles K.
Bowles; Sergeants James Colley, Thos. G. Chilons,   Thos.
Carter, Harman A. Pulliam; Privates Jos. Anderson, Arch'd
Atkinson, Anderson Bowles,   Robt.   Blunhall,   Elkanah A.
Brooks, Joseph Burnard, Thos.   Carver,   Wm.   Childress,
Chas. Colley, Jr., Alex'r. Chisholm Pendleton, R. Childress,
John S. Crutchfield, Richard Childress, Richard Childress,
Jr., Daniel Couch, Spotswood Childress, Theophilus Chewning, John R. Chisholm, Nathaniel W.   Dandridge,   Archibald B. Dandridge, Robert   A. Dandridge,   Allen   Denton,
James Denton, Richard S. Duke, Elisha Ellis, James Glenn,
John Gleen, Jr., William Gleen, John Gentry, Archibald
Glenn, Chapman Gordon, Thomas Hunnicutt, Edward Hatton, Richard Johnson, John B. Jones, Miles B. Lockmane,
Overton Mallory, Thilman   Mallory,   Wm. Moseley, David
Mallory, Richard Morris, Daniel Mitchell,   John   Nuckols,
Wm. Nuckols, Reuben Nuckols, Nathaniel Nuckols, Robt.
Pulliam, Sr., Richard Phillips, Robt. J. Pulliam, Sam'l Pulliam, George S. Pulliam, Joseph Perkins,   Thomas   Pope,
Thomas Richardson, Tolevar Ragland, Wm. Royster, Geo.
Shields, Wm. Shoemaker,   Miles   Taylor, Edward Taylor,
John Taylor,   James Underwood, John Underwood, Shadrack Vaughan, Benj. Vaughan, Wm. Williams, Isham R.
Woodson, Wm. Winston.

The 74th Virginia Regiment, Colonel Wm. Trueheart,
had Capt. Joseph F. Price's company, with the following:
Lieutenant Wm. Day; Ensign Francis Blunt; Sergeants
John Goodwin, John Chesterman, Edward Valentine, Wm.
D. Winston, Walker Taylor; Privates Henry Arnall, Sr.,

Henry Arnall, Jr., Charles D. Alvis, Len P. Anderson, Edmund M. Anderson, Richard Arnall, Lemuel Alvis, Thomas Austin, Joseph Arnall, Davis Arnall, Robert Alvis, John Blunt, Lewis Berkeley, Thomas Bowles, Samuel Busick, Wm. Byars, Michael B. Blankenbiker, Isaac Butler, James Baber, Joseph Blunt, Nelson Brooks, Thos. B. Cosby, Wm. Dabney, John Darracott, Thos. Doswell, Abram W. Davis, Walter C. Day, Miles C. Eggleston, George Eggleston, Jas. Footson, John Grubbs, Sam'l Grantland, Richard Hope, Wm. O. Harris, Wm. Harris, Epaphroditus Howle, Winfield Harris, Richard B. Hendrick, Wm. Hope, Wm. Haines, David Hackney, John Haley, Winston M. Hicks, Johnson Jones, Richard C. B. Jones, Jesse Jones, Jr., Edward W. Kimbrough, James Lowry, Joseph Lane, Solomon Lowry, Sam'l Lowry, Claiborne Lowry, Wm. Luman, Timothy P. R. Lester, Wm. Long, Wm. Lambert, Claiborne Mallory, Wm. Mallory, Wm. Mallory, Jr., Turner Mallory, Fleming Mallory, Stephen Mallory, James May, James M. Morriss, Pleasant Mathiss, Wm. Norvell, Thos. W. Norvell, Mordecai Page, John Patterson, Samuel Patterson, Joseph Patterson, Edmund Patterson, Wm. Pearson, Plummer Potter, Thos. R. Rootes, Arch'd Richardson, Landon Richardson, Nathaniel Stevens, Julius Stephens, John Seddons, Thos. Southward, Simeon Souther, Wm. Sheppard, John Southward, Wm. Shirley, Pleasant Terrell, Anthony Thornton, Wm. D. Taylor, Annistead Thornton, John D. Thilman, Thomas Trevilian, Walker Taylor, Wm. Terrell, Meredith Thacker, George Valentine, Wm. C. Williams, Sam'l Williams, James Winston, Phil B. Winston, John Williams, Jr., Thomas Yarborough, Jesse Yarborough, Elisha Yarborough.

The Seventy-Fourth Virginia Regiment, Colonel Wm. Truehart had Captain Charles Thompson, Jr.; Lieutenant

Edmund Higgason; Ensign Henry H. Jones; Sergeants Michael R. Jones, John Higgason, George S. Netherland, Frederick Shoemaker; Privates Wm. Callis, Wm. Corker, Richard Callis, Dan'l Corker, Wm. S. Dandridge, Gideon Hanes, Martin Hall, Pleasant Hanes, Garland Higgison, Richard Higgason, Christopher Hanes, Sam'l R. Jones, Wm. Mills, Wade Mills, Jackson Mills, Fleming Puryear, David Sims, Jr., Wm. Stanley, Thos. Swift, Chapman Stuard, Richmond Terrell, Wm. A. Thompson, Thos. W. Thacker, Wm. Walton, Jr., Joseph Watson.

The Fourth regiment had a troop of cavalry from Hanover: Captain James Underwood; Lieutenants Arch'd D. Dandridge, Robt. A. Dandridge; Cornet John C. Underwood; Sergeants John King, John G. Childers, Nathaniel W. Dandridge, Joseph Woodson; Corporals Fred Shoemaker, Thos. Elmore, Nath'l Anthony, Jr., Charles Childress; Trumpeter John H. Priddy; Privates Thos. S. Aail, (Vail?) Thos. Atkinson, Robt. S. Austin, Sam'l J. Pulliam, (Pulliam?) Ambrose Brooks, Thos. Bowles, Nath'l Crenshaw, Spotswood Childers, Peter Copeland, Pendleton R. Childress, Ed Cameron, James Denton, Nath'l Dogan, Allen Denton, John England, Wm. Ford, Solomon Harris, Pleasant Hatton, Ed. W. Kimbrough, Alex'r Loving, John Mallory, Jr., John Mann, Overton W. Mallory, Benj. Mann, Nath'l Mills, Stephen Mallory, John Nuckols, Nath'l Nuckols, David Nuckols, John Nash, Ben Perkins, Wm. Sayre, Jesse Sayre, Christian Stone, John H. Taylor, Garland Thompson, Francis Underwood, Rich'd A. Woodson, Reuben Wood.

The Seventy-Fourth Regiment had Captain Hudson M. Wingfield; Lieutenants Wm. Priddy, Wm. Cock; Ensign. Henry A. Timberlake; Sergeants Wm. Timberlake, Francis Starke, Elisha Jones; Privates Fred K. Bowe, Absolom

Browning, Jehu Browning, John C. Brock, Thomas Cross, Wm. Cocke, Hector Davis, Wm. Ford, Robert Hicks, Thos. Hicks, Thomas Hobson, Thos. Kersey, John King Jr., Jas. L. Littlepage, Elijah Priddy, James P. Ragland, John P. Starke, Henry A. Timberlake, Benj. A. Timberlake, Wm. Turner, Thos. Walker, Thos. Wingfield, Joseph Wingfield, John Wingfield, Benj. Wingfield. (See Virginia Muster Roll War 1812, in State Library.)

THE MEXICAN WAR

The records of the Mexican War are inaccessible, and so the names of the brave men who went from Hanover and fought under Taylor and Scott will have to await their publication or until more definite information can be obtained. In my youth I knew one or more of the veterans —one of them being Mr. Jackson, father of Wm. Price Jackson and Wesley Jackson whose descendants are citizens of the county.

The Hanover soldiers in that war as in other wars mentioned gave a good account of themselves, and their heroism is part of the history of the county.

THE WAR BETWEEN THE STATES

Of all the wars, none has ever affected the people of Hanover as did the War between the States. Its causes have been so often told that a repetition of them here is useless.

One party taught that the Constitution of the United States over-rode the rights of the separate states in the matter of secession as well as in that of the question of property, and franchises which had been specifically granted. The other party taught that the separate States had reserved the right of secession which bound all the citizens of such State, when such right so reserved was exercised by the State in its separate and soverign capacity by a constitutional convention. This latter position was held for many years and the book taught at the West Point Military Academy when Robert E. Lee and others of his time studied there, held the latter view of secession. (See Rawle's work on the Constitution Edition of that period.)

As soon as Virginia seceded by act of the Secession Convention on the 17th day of April, 1861, the spirit of separation from the union which had been punctuated by Mr. Lincoln's demand to have the States contribute soldiers to restore the Union, became universal.

Hanover at once replied, and the Patrick Henry Rifles, the Ashland Grays, the Hanover Grays, known later as Company C, E, and I respectively of the fifteenth Virginia Infantry reported for service. These Companies always had a grievance against the Military authorities in Richmond because of their right to have been called the third Regiment instead of the fifteenth. This by reason of their priority in enlistment as volunteers. Such however was the record of the fifteenth Regiment that few except those who remembered the fact had occasion to refer to the matter.

The 56th Virginia Regiment had in it Company K, commanded by Captain D. C. Harrison, a Presbyterian minister who was killed in battle.

The Hanover Troop later became Company G of the famous fourth Virginia Regiment. Its Captain, Williams C. Wickham, was wounded having been promoted to Colonel and afterwards brigadier. Another Captain, Wm. Newton was killed; and its last Captain, D. J. Timberlake was twice wounded.

Perhaps no arm of the service in the Confederacy was more conspicious than the Artillery. And the soldiers from Hanover helped to give it fame.

There were three famous Companies of Artillery from the County:

(1) The Morris Artillery (commanded respectively by Lewis M. Coleman, R. C. M. Page, (of Albemarle) and Chas. R. Montgomery, the first named being mortally wounded at the battle of Fredericksburg.)

(2) The Hanover Artillery commanded by Captain William Nelson and afterwards by Captain G. W. Nelson, the former promoted to Colonel, and the latter captured while on the staff of the Chief of Artillery.

(3) The Ashland Artillery commanded by Captain Pichegru Woolfolk.

In addition to these organized Companies from Hanover the natives of the County dwelling beyond her borders did their part as true citizens and their names are registered in the bronze tablets attached to the beautiful monument at Hanover Court House, to be remembered for their gallant service to their country.

Perhaps no citizen of the county won more fame as an artillery officer than did Lt.-Colonel Hilary J. Jones, so well known as the head of the famous Hanover Academy, and father of our notable Admiral who bears his father's name, and inherited his gallantry.

Soldiers whose names should be on the Monument at the Court House are Vivian M. Fleming, who was a member of the second Richmond Howitzers, Dr. George W. Fleming, of Society Hill, South Carolina, who was on Colonel Lewis M. Coleman's Staff and Mr. Chas. Morris, of Athens, Georgia, who was in the Quartermaster's Department of the government in Richmond.

Hanover men appeared in every great battle of the army of Northern Virginia. It was from the death of one of them at First Manassas, and his burial in the family burying ground at the Fontaine home that Thomas Nelson Page took certain scenes in "Marse Chan."

Hanover, lying as it does between Washington and Richmond, was the scene of much action during the Civil War. "The track of the armies" lay across her borders; for the McClellan Campaign in 1862, and the Grant Campaign of 1864 blazed a wide trail. Besides these great Campaigns, there were the raids of Kilpatrick, Stoneman, and Sheridan.

In the early part of the war, Colonel John S. Mosby was captured at Beaver Dam. He was not so well known and was duly exchanged, as he might not have been a year or so later.

In the spring of 1862, General Joseph E. Johnston, seeing that unless he retired from the peninsula his fate might be that of Cornwallis at Yorktown, withdrew leisurely to the neighborhood of Richmond and fought at Seven Pines (Fair Oaks) a fight, which many believe was a drawn battle because of the wound he received when victory was at hand. On May 11th, 1862, President Davis in writing to General Johnston referred to "the Drooping Cause of Our Country." Stonewall Jackson in the Valley was withholding from McClellan's aid the forces under Fremont, Milroy, Banks, and Shields, as well as the forces under McDowell near Fredericksburg.

On the 11th of June, 1862, General Lee wrote General Jackson telling of sending him fourteen veteran regiments to enable him to crush the forces against him in the Valley, and then directed the leaving of available troops to watch the Country, and guard the passes, etc., and ordering him

with the main body, including those sent, to move rapidly
to Ashland by rail or otherwise as he might find the most
advantageous, and to sweep down between the Chickahominy and Pamunkey, cutting up the enemy's communications while he (Lee) attacked General McClellan in front.

Lee directed Jackson to keep him advised of his move-
ments, and if practicable to precede his troops, so as to
confer and arrange for a simultaneous attack.

On the same day, June 11th, 1862, General Lee sent
General Stuart with about 1,200 cavalry and a battery
of horse artillery to investigate McClellan's right flank, extending almost to Hanover Courthouse.   Stuart's brilliant
performance has been said to set a new mark for cavalry
leaders, the world over.   He set out from Richmond, and
rode North, as if bound for the Mountains.   Then turning
eastward, he passed through Hanover on McClellan's right
driving before him a small body of cavalry found there and
defeating a force occupying "Old Church."   Before reaching this point, Captain Latane was killed leading a charge.
"The burial of Latane" with the service of the church read
by the mistress of "Summerhill" in Hanover is a well
known picture.

Stuart struck McClellan's line of communications
at Tunstall's Station on the Southern Railroad, and then
turned to the Chickahominy in McClellan's rear.
Finding part of the bridge washed away, he supplied timber from an old house nearby and took his men over, making the horses swim.   Reaching the North bank of the
James he swept beyond McClellan's left back to Richmond
(See T. N. Page's Life of Lee, and Mary Johnston's The
Long Roll).

On the 16th of June, 1862, General Lee made a recon-
noissance of the Federal position on the Hanover side of

the Chickahominy, where there were 25,000 men commanded by General Fitz-John Porter. The main body of
his force occupied a position near the Gaines' house, and
one division was posted at Mechanicsville.

On June 25th, 1862, General Jackson was bivouacked
at Ashland. He had expected in his conference with General Lee held in Richmond, to attack early on the 26th.
General Lee's order of battle spoke of Jackson being on
the night of the 25th at Slash Church ready to march at
3 o'clock on the morning of the 26th on the road to Pole
Green to deliver the attack which was to be the signal for
A. P. Hill to cross the Chickahominy at the Meadow
Bridges. (See Lee's order for battle of Mechanicsville.)
Jackson did not reach the field however until 4 o'clock in
the afternoon of the 26th of June. It is "the fly in the
ointment" of that great General's career. So "Mechanicsville" was fought by a costly frontal attack without the
aid of the flank attack which General Lee had planned.

A. P. Hill waited until 3 P. M. on the 26th of June and
crossed into Hanover at the Meadow Bridges, and fought
the battle of Mechanicsville with heavy loss though joined
by Longstreet and D. H. Hill. The next day the battle of
Gaines' Mill was fought with Jackson up and taking gallant part. As McClellan during the next few days
changed his base and crossed the Chickahominy into Henrico, the campaign in Hanover ended.

Lee's well planned scheme to capture McClellan in
Hanover failed, though the people of the County in common with the people of the South breathed freely when it
was known that the invading army had been driven beyond her borders, and compelled to seek refuge under the
shelter of gunboats at Harrison's Landing on James River.

As a little boy, the author saw Jackson's men march

from Beaver Dam towards Ashland on their way to the
seven day fights, and heard the musketry fire and cannon-
ade at Mechanicsville.

At the South Anna Bridge near Hanover Junction,
on June 26th, 1863, Lieutenant-Colonel T. L. Hargrove
and Captain R. L. Rice with Company A 44th N. C. Regiment having 64 men fought for four hours 1,500 mounted
men of Colonel Spears with two field pieces. General
Lee's supplies at Hanover Junction were saved. When the
surrender was finally made, not a Confederate soldier was
on his feet. (Raleigh News and Observer, May 9, 1926.)

Although there was much marching through the County during the other years of the Civil War, the year 1864
saw the great campaign of that year when the genius of
Lee and the gallantry of his army made the Grant campaign dwindle from the magnitude which prompted that
great soldier to write his government that he "would fight
it out on this line if it took all summer," and while his army
was astride the North Anna to inform his government that
"Lee's army was whipped already."

Within a week after Grant had made this declaration,
his army was shattered on the bloody field of Second Cold
Harbor by that "whipped army;" and summer passed and
winter came and spring arrived before starvation as his
ally enabled Grant to receive the surrender of that army at
a point far from the line between Washington and Richmond on which he had proposed to fight it out that summer before.

The details of the 1864 campaign in Hanover are full
of interest. While the two armies in the month of May
were fighting in the Spotsylvania Campaign, Sheridan
came into the County on the 10th of May following, and
burned Beaver Dam, where General Lee's supplies were,

and then started for Richmond, via Trinity Church, Negrofoot and Ground Squirrel Bridge. He got as far as Yellow Tavern, when he found across his path Stuart with
Wickham's brigade on the right, and Lomax on the left
—Fitz Lee.

It is thought by some that Richmond was saved when
Wickham's brigade struck Sheridan at Jarrold's Mill, and
drove him from the Telegraph Road to the road leading to
Beaver Dam. Stuart rode into Hanover at Davenport's
Bridge over the North Anna and rode by "Beaver Dam"
home of the Fontaines, where his wife and children were.
His troops having reached Beaver Dam Station, just after
Sheridan left by the route above mentioned, Stuart sent
Gordon's brigade to follow along the Mountain Road,
while he with Fitz Lee's two brigades marched to Hanover Junction (Doswell) where after a little rest, his
force pushed on at 1 o'clock in the morning along the Telegraph Road to Yellow Tavern, six miles from Richmond.

A fight occurred in the town of Ashland and the enemy
was driven out by the 2nd Virginia Cavalry. (See life of
Stuart by H. B. McClellan.) On the 28th of May, 1864,
there was a fight at Haw's Shop in the lower end of the
County and was part of the Grant campaign.

Markers have been placed in many localities to preserve the record of actions in Hanover. So far these have
been placed so as to mark the campaigns in lower Hanover.
They embrace all points of interest east of the Telegraph
Road and between the Totopotomoi and the Chickahominy—at Mechanicsville, Beaver Dam Creek, and beyond where the Federal line was, at Walnut Grove Church,
two near New Cold Harbor, one at Dr. Gaines', and one
at the Watt's home.

The markers at Second Cold Harbor are to be at Lin-

ney's Corner, Enon Church, Hanovertown, and where Latane was killed. Breastworks on the South Anna where
the Chesapeake & Ohio Railway crosses mark a gallant
defense at that point, already mentioned.

War Incidents

There are many interesting incidents connected with
the war in Hanover. Space here forbids extended mention. General Stuart, on his ride around McClellan, rode
at night with a courier to "Hickory Hill" to see Colonel
Wickham who was there suffering from a wound received
in the Peninsular. A citizen of the county then a lad
sleeping in his father's room was called that he might see
and speak to General Stuart.

Some Federal officers who saw Thomas Nelson Page
and other little boys on the roadside, as they charged by,
told them it was no place for boys, and they must get away
as a fight was about to begin.

As General Lee sat writing at a little table at his tent
door, Jo Lane Stern then acting as telegraph operator at
Doswell, finding that the General did not look up, put his
hand on the General's shoulder to let him know that he
had a telegram for him.

Andrew Ellerson as a boy sent to guide some troops
by a certain route told General Lee a cat couldn't cross
the swamp at that point, and when some days later he rode
with General Lee by the place, he could not forbear to say
to him "Look General, this is the place you wanted me to
lead those men across!"

Lincoln Sydnor told Ellerson that when he was acting
as guide to General Jackson across the Totopotomoi and
missed the road, General Ewell wanted to hang him, and
that his life was saved by General Jackson. General Wm.

H. F. Lee was captured by Federal troops at "Hickory Hill" and taken away, though desperately wounded. His younger brother, Robert, escaped capture by hiding in the box trees in the yard.

In Major H. B. McClellan's Life of General Stuart the following incident of a Hanover soldier is cited as a parallel to another mentioned on the Federal side. When the cavalry charged Averell's force after they had crossed the Rapidan river at Kelley's Ford, a fence obstructed the way. Sergeant W. J. Kimbrough of Company G, 4th Virginia Cavalry, had been wounded early in the action. He refused to leave the field, and in the last charge was the first to spring to the ground to throw down the fence which obstructed the way. Remounting he dashed on to the head of his regiment, was twice sabered over the head, had his arm shattered by a bullet, was captured and carried over the river, but made his escape, and on the same night walked back twelve miles to the camp of his regiment.

General Jackson as he rode in 1862 to Richmond for an interview with General Lee stopped for rest at "North River" where lived Mr. Henry Carter, whose family at that time were away from home. He asked for a table and began to write. Then he took his shoes off, and said to his host, "You go to bed, I shall leave here during the night." In the morning the chairs and table "were put to rights," and Jackson had passed through Hanover to confer with Lee. On the same march he rested at noon at William R. Winn's home near "Gwathmey."

At another point on the road General Jackson and a member or members of his staff stopped for a drink of water by a well where a woman was drawing water. Noticing how the young men handed the officer the little cher before any of them drank, she recognized who he was,

DR. HENRY ROSE CARTER.

poured the water out that was left in the pitcher and started to the house. "Give us some water!—they called after her. "All right!" she replied, but nobody esle shall ever drink out of General Jackson's Pitcher!"

That pitcher is somewhere in Hanover to this day.

The Monument.

On the monument at Hanover Courthouse are the names of Hanover men who were in service of the Confederacy. These names are set in bronze and give the arm of the service and the organizations. Under the heading "Other Commands," are the names of those who were residents of the county when they enlisted elsewhere.

The monument carries on one face the legend:— "Hanover—To Her Confederate Soldiers and To Her Noble Women Who Loved Them. 1861-'65;" and the names of officers above the rank of lieutenant." Note: (d) means died in service; (w) means wounded; (k) means killed.

Such officers were: Wms. C. Wickham, Brig. Gen'l. (w); D. C. Harrison, Colonel (k); Geo. W. Richardson, Colonel; H. W. Wingfield, Colonel; Lewis M. Coleman, Lt. Colonel (k); H .P. Jones, Lt. Colonel; Wm. Nelson, Colonel (w); Wm. B. Newton, Lt. Colonel (k); C. St. Geo. Noland, Lt. Colonel; H. St. Geo. Tucker, Lt. Colonel (d); R. T. Ellett, Major; John B. Fontaine, Major (k); Peter Fontaine, Major (w); John Page, Major; Phil Sutton, Major; L. Frank Terrell, Major (d); Chas. W. Dabney, Captain; Theodore S. Garnett, Captain; J. C. Govers, Captain (w); John P. Harrison, Captain (d); C. R. Montgomery, Captain; Geo. W. Nelson, Captain W. B. Talley, Captain; D. A. Timberlake, Captain (2w); J. D. Waid, Captain; Phil. B. Winston, Captain; Pichegru Woolfolk, Captain.

The cavalry had the "Hanover Troop" which became Company G of the 4th Virginia Regiment. Besides the officers named W. C. Wickham, W. B. Newton and D. A. Timberlake, there were the following: O. C. Anderson, Corporal (k), H. S. Anderson, S. D. Anderson, J. C. Anthony (d), Sam M. Baker, J. S. Benson, Wm. J. Binford (w), A. C. Blake, J. S. Blanton, R. F. Blanton, J. H. Blunt, Wm. F. Blunt (2w), B. W. Bowe, J. W. Bowe, B. H. Bowles, 2nd Lt. (k); A. W. Brock (w), G. G. Brown (w), J. A. Brown, J. B. Brown (w), J. C. Bullock, T. Butler, W. E. Carter, Wm. J. Carpenter, E. A. Catlin, R. Chewning, J. W. Childress, J. A. Chisholm, G. H. Clarke, J. C. Cooke (w), J. Mc. P. Cooke, B. F. Corr, G. W. Cosby, C. A. Crump, John J. Crutchfield, J. L. Dietrick, C. H. Day, B. T. Doswell, T. B. Dunn, Chas. T. Dyson, A. R. Ellerson, L. Ellis, J. T. Ellett, W. H. Ellett, T. H. Ellett, L M. Estes, Edmund Fontaine, Sergeant (k); C. Fontaine, Jno. B. Fontaine, Surgeon (k); Peter Fontaine (w), J. C. Gilman (w), J. R. Gilman (w), T. E. Gilman (w), G. D. Glinn, G. Green, Chas. P. Goodall, Surgn., J. L. Green, M. M. Green, J. T. Grubbs, E. Harris, J. Harris, R Harris (k), W. T. Huffman, C. H. Jenkins, A. C. Jones W. J. Kimbrough, Sergeant (k); G. W. King, Corpl., J. R. Lawrence, W. Q. Lawrence, J. E. Leadbetter (w), P. H. Leadbetter, R. Lowry, J. H. Meredith, M. M. Middlebrooks, J. Moore, A. S. Nash, B. F. Nash, J. W. Nash (k), W. F. Nash, J. R. Norment, A. B. Nuckols, P. H Nuckols, A. J. Nuckols (k), E. G. Nuckols, J. H. Nuckols, B. J. Nuckols (k), S. R. Nuckols (w), E. T. Payne, C. Patman, W. F. Patman, W. Patman, Lieutenant; E. Payne, W. G. Poindexter, W. A. Poindexter, B. C. Pollard, Corpl (k); Wm. Price, R. L. Prddy, (k), E. M. Redd (w), T. J. Sadler, R D. Saunders (k), P. G. Spindle (k), J. T. Stanley, T. J. Stanley, J K. Starke,

Sergeant (w); A. C. Stone, J. L. Sydnor (w), G. B. Sydnor (w), T. W. Sydnor, Lieutenant (2w); T. J. Taliaferro, J. L. Talley, R. W. Talley, C. A. Taylor (w), C. A. Taylor, C. D. Taylor (w), T. F. Taylor, Lieutenant, J. D. Terrell, J. J. Terry (2w), G. N. Thompson (w), R. A. Thornton, J. H. Timberlake, J. L. Timberlake, J. L. Timberlake, J. M. Toler, D. E. Toler, R. C. Tomlin (Stuart's Staff) (k); J. B. Vaughan, J. W. Vaughan, A. A. Was'a, D. F. Waldrop, M. A. Waldrop (w), A. W. Wingfield, C. R. Wingfield (3w), I. W. Wingfield (k), J. A. Wingfield, S. A. Wingfield, P. W. Wingfield, W. L. Wingfield, Sergeant (w); E. P. Winston, Sergeant; R. M. Winston (d), T. Winston, F. E. Wright, J. B. Yarborough.

Cavalry

Other Commands:

F. F. Anderson, J. M. Anderson, Corporal; D. Banker, J. Barker, W. M. Binford (k); T. Bowles, W. Bowles, L. Brown, G. Burnett, W. Burnett, W. Burnett, Hill Carter (w), T. P. Carver, J. W. Crenshaw, J. F. Cross, F. Davis, W. H. Davis, I. Frazier, B. Gouldin, W. Hardin, H. Hooper, J. W. Hoskins, C. Jones (k), J. A. Kelley, N. T. Lipscomb, Jr., G. Livesay, I. Martin, G. W. McAlister, N. C. McGee, C. H. Mills, C. M. B. Mitchell, J. P. Montgomery, L. N. Nash, W. A. Pollard, R. T. Puller (k), E. T. Redd, S. C. Redd (w), W. Saunders, J. O. Sitman, B. Smith, G. Starke, J. Z. Terrell, W. J. Tinsley, A. T. Timberlake (k), A. R. Timberlake, Lieutenant; J. Timberlake, R. W. Timberlake, W. A. Timberlake (k), J. W. Toler (k), E. A. Tomkies, T. B. Trevilian, C. Tyler (k), A. White, C. White (k), T. White, H. Winston, P. B. Winston (Captain on Rosser's Staff), J. L. Woodson, M. R. Woodson.

The Infantry from Hanover had the Patrick Henry Rifles, which became Company C of the Fifteenth Virginia Infantry. Besides the officers mentioned (Captains Chas. W. Dabney and G. B. Swift) there were G. Anthony, J. H. Barley, C. Beale, Landon C. Berkley, 2nd Lieutenant; R. S. Blaycock (k); J. L. Blunt, G. W. Bourne, P. T. Bowles, Lieutenant; T. H. Bourne, W. E. Bowles, Corporal; J. S. Brown, Sergeant (2w); Thad. C. Brown, T. J. Brown, B. B. Bumpass, Corporal (w); T. G. Bumpass, 1st Lieutenant (w); J. W. Bumpass (w), W. N. Bumpass (k), G. C. Butler, J. C. Butler (k), S. M. Butler, J. Cardwell, J. Childress, C. H. Childress, E. V. Chisholm, J. A Chisholm, J. Conner, J. W. Cottrell, M. C. Crenshaw, J. H. Crew, F. P. Dabney, B. F. Davis, J. K. Donahoe, L. P. Duke, J. R. Eddleton (k), U. D. Foster (k), W. Glenn, W. G. Goodman (w), C. W. Hall, J. W. Hall (k), J. S. Hall, W. P. Hall (k), W. G. Hardin, J. J. Harlow, T. M. Hargrove, T. B. Harlow, J. J. Harris, J. P. Harris, W. A. Harris, W. F. Hart, C. R. Holdman (d), P. J. Isbell, J. W. Jackson (k), J. C. W. Jackson, G. N. Jarvis, G. W. Johnson, C. W. Jones, D. L. Jones, J. E. Jones (w), M. L. Jones, T. P. Jones, M. Korb, J. H. Keen, Sr.; D. Kimbrough, L. R. Kimbrough, Sergeant, J. W. Kimbrough Corporal; M. V. B. Lambert (k), T. A. Layne, E. Leadbetter, T. Lipscomb, T. M. Lowry, Sergeant (k), F. F. Mallory, M. M. Mallory (k), T. S. Mallory, G. E. Massie, J. L. Motley, B. Mills, J. W. Moore, J. W. Moody, J. W. B. Newton, A. B. Nuckols, John Page, 1st Sergeant; J. Pollard, E. H. Pollard, Z. L. Pulliam, W. Reynolds (d), P. B. Snead, E. J. Snead, E. J. Snead, E. S. Snead, J. B. Snead (k), R. J. Snead, J. A. Smith, G. K. Stanley, J. F. Stanley, R. S. Stanley, Corporal (w); A. F. Stone (w), J. K. Strong, J. Sullivan, E. B. Talley (k), W. Talley, G. W. Thompson, Corporal (2w); N. B. Thompson (k), T. S. Thompson, W. J. Thompson, J. G. Tiller, Corporal (w); L. S. Tiller, R. E. Tiller, J. H. Tiller, R. W. Toler, R. T. Wash. W. D. Winston (k), W. A. Woodson, J. H. Yarborough.

The Infantry from Hanover had (2) The Ashland Grays, which became Company E of the Fifteenth Virginia Infantry. Besides the officers mentioned (Captains H. St. Geo. Tucker (d), and J. C. Govers (2w), there were W. R. Andrew, J. R. Baker, Corporal (k); T. J. Barnett (w), J. E. Beadles, R. J. Blackwell (d), J. F. Blackwell (w), H. K. Broyles (k), J. H. Bridges, R. J. Brooks, J. H. Buckley, C. H. Buchanan, J. M. B. Buchanan, T. J. Buchanan, R. Bumpass, C. M. Butler, W. Butler (d), E. F. Childress (w), W. J. Childress, W. H. Chisholm, J. C. Collins, W. J. Daniels, 2nd Lieutenant (k); J. C. Dick, Corporal; C. W. Dick, T. A. Deitrick, W. T. Farmer (w), R. J. Farloin, Sergeant (w), E. S. Francis (k), C. R. Francis, J. T. Francis, J. T. B. Francis (w), S. O. Glazebrook, L. W. Glazebrook, 2nd Lieutenant; C. V. Glazebrook, R. L. Green (k), W. Haines (w), J. H. Harris, G. E. Heath, F. H. Hendrick, G. W. Hudgins, W. A. Huffman, J. E. James (k), J. S. James, W. E. James, J. G. Jenkins, C. B. Jones, T. B. Jones, J. E. Jones (w), R. F. Jones, H. C. Jones, 1st Lieutenant (w); G. W. Kelley, G. King, Sergeant; C. Y. Lain, 1st Lieutenant (k); M. Lambert (d), R. L. Lawrence, W. J. Lawrence, J. C. Lively, T. C. Lowry (w), J. M. Luck (k), J. Lumpkin, J. V. McAllister (w), A. S. McDowell (w), A. M. McMurdo, J. W. Mallory, L. E. Mallory, Corporal; J. Perry, J. Prior, W. Smith (d), A. B. Snead, T. M. Snead, W. L. Snead (k), J. H. Stone, R. Stone, W. Stone, G. L. Swift, O. J. Swift, Sergeant; C. C. Taylor, 3rd Lieutenant; C. H. Taylor, 1st Lieutenant; J. P. Thomas (w), W. D. Truel, C. Terrell (k), J. A. Vass, J. P. Vass, T. J. Vass,

Corporal; C. M. White, C. E. Wingfield, W. Wingfield, T. G. Winn (w), J. B. Wood, W. H. Wood, Corporal; J. J. Woodson (k), J. H. Woodson (w), R. R. Woodson, W. H. Woodson, W. K. Woodson, Sergeant (w), J. O. Wright, 2nd Lieutenant.

The Infantry had (3) The Hanover Grays, which became Company I of the Fifteenth Virginia Infantry. Besides the officers mentioned (Captains B. W. Talley and J. D. Waid) there were W. J. Alexander, J. B. Allen, R. Allen, H. C. Atkins, W. T. Atkins, D. B. Benson, C. Batkins (k), W. Bowles, G. C. Boyd, 2nd Lieutenant; W. R. Boyd, 2nd Lieutenant; L. Brown, G. W. Brown, P. H. Brown, E. T. Burch, M. L. Burton, J. M. Butler, C. Carlton, L. M. Cooke (k), J. G. Corbin, J. O. Cosby (w), H. B. Christian, E. P. Crump, A. Curtis, J. W. Davidson, 2nd Lieutenant (k); J. H. Dunn (k), C. Dunn (k), H. C. Dunn, R. S. Dunn (2w), T. Ellett (w), T. Foster, 1st Lieutenant; W. Gaines, R. E. Gardner, J. T. Gibson, R. H. Gibson, J. Gary (w), R. R. Griffin, J. W. Harwood, J. H. Haw, Sergeant; George P. Haw, 1st Lieutenant (w); R. W. Haw, 1st Corporal (w); Edwin Haw (w), Wm. Haw, Sergeant (2w); A. Hazelgrove (d), W. Hogan, R. R. Horne, R. R. Horne (d), W. Hott, P. H. Hughes (w), P. L. Johnson, W. Jones (d), W. W. Jones (w), J. S. Kelley, G. W. Kent (w), H. Lipscomb, B. Longan, W. Mantlo (2w), C. Mantlo (w), J. T. Mills, J. S. Mosby, W. E. Normant, L. M. Nunnaly, T. Otey, W. Otey (w), W. M. Parsley, 2nd Lieutenant; J. W. Pate, W. B. Pate, B. Richardson, J. H. Richardson, H. Richardson (k), W. N. Short, W. H. Smith, Corporal (w); W. C. Smith (k), J. Southard (w), W. Taliaferro, J. A. Talley (k), E. S. Talley (k), W. Talley (d), W. Talley (w), C. A. Talley, P. Thacker, R. H. Thomas, R. A. Thomas, J. Timberlake, J. H. Tomlin, D. L. Tyler, A. J. Via, W. H. Via, J. B. Warren (d),

L. White, 1st Sergeant (k); W. Wicker (k), G. W. Wright, J. J. Wright (w), S. Wright (d), C. Wyatt, W. P. Wyatt.

The Infantry from Hanover had (4), The Harrison Guards, which became Company K of the Fifty-sixth Virginia Infantry. Besides the officer mentioned (Captain D. C. Harrison (k)) there were E. Acree (d), J. Adams (w), W. T. Adams, C. Alexander, A. G. Allison, D. Anderson, W. Barley (w), W. N. Barker, Sergeant; L. Brown, M. Carlton, 2nd Lieutenant (w); W. Chadwick, P. H. Clopton, Lieutenant; C. B. Cox, H. C. Earnest, J. A. Fields (w), W. B. Foster, A. Gathwright (k), B. Gathwright, P. Gathwright, B. C. Hanna, W. G. Harrison, L. Heath, W. F. Higgins, G. D. Hogan, J. H. Hundley, W. Ingram, T. Jackson, H. G. Jefferies, Corporal (w); A. Jenkins, S. Jeter, J. S. Jones, 1st Lieutenant (d); B. Kelley (w), E. W. Kelley (w), H. P. Kelley, W. Livesey, E. Longan, 2nd Lieutenant (w. d); F. Marshall, Corporal (w); J. D. Martin (d), A. M. Martin, Corporal; W T. Martin (w), J. Mason, J. L. McGhee (w), P. C. McGhee, W. A. McGhee, Corporal (w); A. McGregor, P. D. Moore, 2nd Lieutenant; E. M. Peace (w), W. H. Peace (d), G. Puller, R. Richardson (d), W. T. Richardson, W. E. Talley, Lieutenant; H. Tate, T. P. Temple, G. Thacker, P. Thacker, T. Trueman (k), B. H. Tucker, Sergeant (3w); H. T. Tucker, Sergeant (w); J. Tucker (w), J. E. Tucker, J. T. Tucker, E. Via (2w), H. Via (w), W. F. Waldrop, F. Warren (d), W. White (d), W. Wicker, W. H. Wood, G. W. Woody, P. J. Woody (d), H. Wright (w).

Those in "Other Commands" of Infantry were J. E. Acree (k), G. Anderson (k), C. H. Atkinson, W. H. Basket, L. Blackburn (k), W. Blake, G. Blanton (k), H. C. Bowe, N. W. Bowe, Sergeant; W. N. Catlin, G. Chewning, W. T. Christian, T. B. Crenshaw, B. K. Cocke, Lieutenant (w);

S. Coleman, H. C. Cross, R. T. Darracott, J. L. Dyson, M. T. Eddleton, C. Farmer, J. M. Finn, R. M. Fontaine, P. H. Ford, M. Gary (k), D. Gentry (w), J. C. Jentry, A. Glenn (w), I. Glenn, J. T. Harris, W. H. Harris, R. Hazelgrove, H. Hill (w), E. Hill (w), J. E. Hott, A. V. Irby (w), E. W. Jackson, P. Jenkins, D. Johnson, G. A. Jones (w), P. Kersey, R. Kersey, J. King, W. Long, J. W. Loving, C. Martin, J. Martin, O. F. McDowell, D. Melton, H. Mettert, W. T. Mills, C. L. C. Minor, 1st Lieutenant; D. B. Moore (k), J. W. Noel, N. B. Noland, W. Oliver, J. Owens, J. F. Page, J. P. Perrin, Sergeant (k); S. Perrin, A. E. Pollard (k), E. Priddy, Corporal (w); W. G. Puller, E. C. Puryear, C. M. Redd, J. T. Redd, Sergeant; J. Richardson, E. Ruffin, S. M. Shelton, W. P. Shelton (w), C. M. Sitman, H. D. Sitman (d), J. Sizer, L. R. Smith (k), L. R. Smith (k), W. Smith, W. E. Snead (d), C. Spencer (d), D. Stanley, W. Stanley, G. T. Stone, W. Sydnor, Sergeant; F. Tate, J. Q. Terrell, W. A. Thomas (w), W. H. Tinsley, J. Travers, C. H. Vaughan, J. Wade, M. F. Waldrop, T. Nash, N. F. Wheat (w) C. White, J. C. Wilkinson, I. A. Wingfield, J. A. Wingfield, L. R. Wingfield (w), J. M. Wingfield (k), S. L. Wingfield, W. R. Winn, C. R. Woodson.

The Artillery from Hanover (besides the officers mentioned, Captains L. M. Coleman (k) and C. R. Montgomery, and R. C. M. Page, of Albemarle) had The Morris Artillery, variously known as Coleman's, Page's, and Montgomery's Battery. In it were: O. J. Armstrong, S. Baker (d), M. Baker (d), J. Barker (d), W. H. Barlett, R. Barrett, J. T. Baughan, J. C. Browning (k), W. S. Browning, A. W. Brooks (d), J. A. Brooks, W. H. Brooks, R. M. Bullock, J. S. Bumpass (w), J. F. Butler, J. G. Butler, R. F. Butler (d), W. T. Butler, C. L. Coleman, 2nd Lieutenant (k); W. J. Chapman (d), J. W. Chewning, J. O.

Chisholm (d), W. I. Chisholm, Corporal (w), J. B. Collins, J. H. Cross (w), N. A. Cross (d), R. H. Cross (w), R. F. Davis, M. C. Dickinson, F. H. Duke, A. G. Duke, J. W. Eddleton (d), F. Elmer (k), J. C. England, R. B. Eubank (w), G. J. Foster, J. T. Fleming, W. T. Grubbs, U. Grymes, J. F. Hall (w), S. W. Hall, J. D. Hardgrove, A. J. Harris (k), E. M. Harris (k), T. J. Harris, Corporal (w); B. A. Hazelgrove (w), T. Harper, C. P. Higginson, Lieutenant; E. P. Holloway (w), P. A. Howle, Corporal; Wm. P. Jackson, R. T. James (w), H. P. Jones, Lieutenant; T. L. Jones, Corporal (d); V. R. Jones, A. J. Lambert (k). W. T. Lambert, A. Lane (w), F. T. Lane, J. G. Lane (d), J. H. Lane (w), J. W. Lane, A. T. Leitch, J. H. Leitch, Corporal (d); G. B. Leitch, G. A. Leitch (w), W. L. Lumpkin, Sergeant; B. F. Lowry, M. C. Lowry (d), J. V. Lowry, W. L. Luck (d), P. W. Luck (k), M. Madison, J. T. Mallory (w), L. L. Mallory, E. W. Morris, 1st Lieut. — — Massie, Lieutenant; J. O. McGhee (k), A. J. Mills, J. T. Mills, W. J. Mills, B. D. Mitchell, T. McDaniel, Sergeant; A. W. Nuchols, J. A. H. Oliver, L. Page (w), J. Pate, I. S. Patterson, M. Patterson (w), P. H. Patterson, W. Patterson (d), T. S. Penn, E. T. Perkins, N. Perkins, J. H. Phillips, J. S. Pleasants (w), J. F. Rice, Z. J. Rice, J. M. Sacra, A. Smith (k), A. F. Southworth (w), J. S. Southworth, W. D. Southward, W. G. Southward, S. M. Southard, W. T. Southard, T. A. Spicer, B. F. Stanley (w), G. Stanley, H. B. Stanley, J. F. Stanley, L. C. Stanley, T. T. Stanley (w), W. S. Stanley, B. H. Stone (k), C. S. Stone, Sergeant (k); J. Stone (k), S. M. Stone, Corporal; W. A. Terrell, A. H. Thacker (w), B. F. Thacker, H. T. Thacker, Corporal; S. Thacker (k), J. L. Thompson, Sergeant (w); G. W. Tiller (w), C. Timberlake (w), W. T. Timberlake (w), J. F. Tinsley, W.

W. Toller, H. W. Toller, Lieutenant (k); F. Tyler, F. Tyler, H. J. C. Vass, J. E. Wash (w), H. L. West, J. F. West, L. West, J. M. White (w), M. White, A. J. Wiltshire, B. F. Wiltshire, J. Wiltshire (d), J. M. Wickham (w), C. D. Woody (w), T. F. Woody (d), W. T. Yarborough (d).

Besides the officers mentioned (Wm. Nelson and Geo. W. Nelson, Captains) there were in the Hanover Artillery: M. M. Anderson, C. M. Anderson (d), E. M. Anderson (k), H. R. Berkeley, J. H. Berkeley, J. L. Berkeley (w), T. H. Bourne, Charles Cooke, 1st Lieutenant; J. C. Corker (w), J. F. Corker, L. W. Duke, T. Duke, 3rd Lieutenant; J. W. Durvin, R. L. Fleming, W. S. Flippo, B. B. Graves, J. Graves, J. D. Gilson, J. Farmer (d), Wm. M. Fontaine, 1st Lieutenant; G. Grimes, J. O. Grimes, W. Grimes, T. S. Garnett, Jr. (Stuart's Staff); J. Haines (d), C. M. Hall, G. W. Hall, W. W. Hall, F. Hall, T. S. Hall, J. H. Hall, M. Hall, W. E. Harris, B. F. Harris (k), S. Harris (k), J. Harris (d), A. J. Holloway, E. Jackson. A. W. Jackson, L. Lowry, R. E. Lowry, E. D. Lowry, S. F. Luck (d), S. Mills (w), J. T. Mills, R. V. Mason (w), Phil. S. Mosby, H. G. Mallory, F. L. Maddox, —. Miller, J. Murphey (k), A. B. Nuchols, A. N. Nuchols, R. C. Nelson (d), J. E. Oliver (d), P. O'Brien, Phil. O'Brien, E. Parrish, J. Perkins, T. Perkins (d), J. Perkins (w), G. W. Perkins, R. Perkins, C. L. Ragland, P. W. Ragland, Wm. Ronquist, E. Rowzey, S. H. C. Sims, B. L. Smith. J. Stone, H. Shelbourne, J. S. Southard, J. Snead, R. H. Spicer, R. Stringfellow, H. M. Stringfellow, 2nd Lieutenant; S. C. Sydnor (d), J. H. Terrell, N. B. Terrell, B. B. Turner (d), T. C. Turner (d), E. Taylor, F. S. Terry. W. H. Terry, C. R. Thompson, J. L. Thompson (w), A. J. Thacker, R. R. Tyler, E. S. Wash, Robt. B. Winston (w), G. S. Wright, Dabney Williamson (w).

The Artillery from Hanover had the Ashland Artillery.
Besides the officer mentioned (Captain Pichegru Wool-
folk) there were: R. L. Atkinson, B. F. Bryce, E. S.
Bumpass, F. Bumpass, G. W. Bumpass (d), J. E. Butler
(w), W. E. Butler, P. A. Cason, S. Chandler, Corporal; J.
W. Chrismas, L. A. Eddleton, W. H. England (k), B. Z.
Furry, J. Ford, J. B. Gardner, 2nd Lieutenant, W. A. Gayle,
J. H. Gillespie, J. T. Harris (w), J. R. Harris, J. Hancock,
J. W. Hancock, R. E. Hancock, A. E. Higginson, 2nd Lieu-
tenant; F. W. Hope, W. H. Jenkins (w), A. J. Johnson,
L. Johnson, J. R. Kent, J. R. Lowry, B. Mallory, C. J.
Mallory, T. B. Mallory, W. T. Mills, B. Meredith, 1st Lieu-
tenant (k), T. B. Moody (k), I. Mosby (k), E. Moran, A. C.
Nunnaly, A. Poindexter, J. E. Poindexter, J. E. Patterson,
W. J. Saunders, Corporal; W. G. Sims, J. T. Southard (w),
W. A. Tate, F. B. Taylor, F. W. Taylor, J. H. Terrell, J. R.
Terrell (k), N. Terrell, Sergeant; W. D. Terrell, 2nd Lieu-
tenant (w); C. J. Terrell, 2nd Lieutenant; J. W. Thacker,
G. D. Vaughan, Jr., 1st Lieutenant; E. T. Woolfolk, J.
Woolfolk.

"Other Commands" in the Artillery had: J. H. Ander-
son, L. C. Anderson, R. Anderson (k), R. P. Anderson (k),
S. M. Armstrong (w), C. Arnold, J. J. Atkinson, R. Atkin-
son, S. L. Atkinson, R. H. Baker, F. Baker, V. Baker, R.
C. Barker (k), J. Bowles, A. Brooks, W. Burnett, J. J.
Burton (k), J. E. Butler, G. Carlton, J. R. Cason, T. W.
Cauthorn, C. P. Cross, C. R. Darracott, G. T. Darracott, J.
V. Darracott, W. T. Darracott (d), J. Edwards, J. Ellis, R.
T. Ellett, A. C. Gibson, W. Gilman, A. Glass (d), T. Glass,
H. B. Grubbs (2w), W. Grubbs, E. G. Gwathmey, M.
Harris, S. Harris, W. H. Harris, J. P. Harrison (d), J.
R. Haw, W. J. Hall, J. W. Hall (d), W Heath, W. H.
Hughes, W. Hughes, W. Jarvis, H. S. Jones, 1st Lieu-

tenant (k); L. Jones, Sergeant; P. L. Jones, W. Jones (k), W. W. Jones, 1st Lieutenant; W. Kelley, L. M. King, J. B. Lipscomb, C. A. Mallory, R. W. Mallory, B. Marks, A. C. Martin, G. D. Martin, P. Martin, W. Meredith, Corporal (k); W. Meredith (k), Berkeley Minor, B. J. Nuchols (d), T. Nuchols, H. J. W. Perkins, A. Pate (k), T. M. Perkins, S. Perrin (d), J. Perrin (k), B. F. Pleasants, J. G. Pleasants, J. E. Poindexter, A. L. Redd, C. P. Slaughter (k), J. C. Slaughter (k), S. H. Slaughter (k), G. Smith, G. Smith (k), J. L. Smith, S. Smith, C. Stewart, Sullens, W Sullivan (k), R. T. Sydnor, W. J. Sydnor, Sergeant; E. F. Thompson, W. Thompson, J. G. Tinsley, A. J. Tomkies (2w), T. W. Tomkies, J. Wade, T. F. Waldrop, E. Wicker (k), J. Wingfield, J. D. Winston, D. Wright (k), T Wright, W. Wright, C. Wright.

Unveiling Monument

On August 27, 1914, there was held at Hanover Court House one of the most notable meetings ever held in the county. It was on the occasion of the unveiling of the monument containing in bronze the names of the soldiers from the county.

The meeting was called to order by Judge Richard H. Cardwell, who called Mr. George P. Haw, President of the Association, to the chair. In the absence of Dr. James Power Smith, who was unavoidably detained, the opening prayer was offered by the Rev. Dr. Frank Page. There was singing by the school children, who had been drilled for the purpose by the ladies of the county. A history of the movement and the work done by the committees of the citizens in raising funds and in securing an accurate list of names of Hanover Soldiers was read by Rosewell Page, Clerk of the Monument Committee. The report of

Mrs. Henry T. Wickham, Treasurer, was read. Mr. Haw presented the Monument in the name of the Association to the Board of Supervisors, and it was received by the Chairman of the Board.

Colonel Robert E. Lee, of Fairfax, was the orator. It is enough to say that the oration was worthy of the occasion.

Familiar as he was with the history of the war, of the Hanover soldiers, the orator's name, descent, and eloquence, combined to thrill the great audience as he recounted the deeds of heroism by those whose names were recorded in the memorial bronze, but more imperishably in the hearts of all Southerners.

The following poem was read by the author:

Soldiers, who still survive your country's call,
   No bugle sounds today the battle cry;
For peace attends you and no tears must fall;
   The dead upon the field had victory.

Fighting for freedom, how they fought and fell,
   And rose again, again resolved to die;
Now we are here in lasting bronze to tell
   The names that put on immortality.

Filled are the annals with your deeds well done,
   When youth and age in rival action wrought;
When son to father, father unto son,
   Displayed the valour, love of country taught.

Furled is your flag; your cause is counted lost,
   Your deeds declared by some of no avail;
Yet of your sacrifice, and of its cost
   This monument doth tell the tragic tale.

Pilgrim and traveler here shall read the roll
  Unveiled for future years to see
How many sons—indeed a glorious toll!
  Our County gave for love—not victory.

THE WORLD WAR

When the World War came the citizens of Hanover were a happy and contented people. There were few very poor, and fewer very rich people.

The effect of the declaration of war upon the life of the people was immediately noticeable. The Draft Act became at once the subject of intense interest to every family in the county. Groups of people were to be seen at every public place—store, church, school, cross roads, mill, or railway station. Upon their faces was an expression of seriousness, unusual and unnatural.

Then came the appointment of the Draft officers, to whom was committed the grave and important duty of determining who was a fit soldier. So well was this work done that the officials who determined the question, which so affected the whole county, have been since the war returned to their former positions by an overwhelming popular vote. Not that there was always satisfaction with the action of the Draft Board; for there were numerous appeals to the Appellate Board in Richmond; but there was always such evident honesty in the action and conduct of the enquiry, so material to the individual and to the State, and everything was so openly and publicly done that even those most affected by the Board's action had to admit its honesty and sincerity.

There were few appeals from the action of the local Board and few of such appeals were successful.

In most cases, such appeals were asked at the instance of friends or family. A father came with a fine up-standing young soldier who was already at Camp Lee, and urged a friend to go with him to try to induce the Appellate Board to discharge the young fellow.

"Why," said he, "that boy has seventy barrels of corn in the field, and not a soul to gather it." After suggesting that the best thing to do would be to get the boy a few days' furlough to gather the crop, the young soldier was asked if he wanted to get out of the army. Looking at his father in a pathetic way, he said "No!" Then the friend said to the father, "Look at him! See how well he looks! Let him stay! He's worth more than a field of corn!"

The result was that the father abandoned the idea of applying for a release. The soldier went to France and came back, and still cultivates the corn field that has never yielded so well as it did that war-year.

After war was declared on the Spring day in 1917 (April 6) by America against Germany, which consisted in the Declaration that a state of war existed on the part of Germany, the County became at once a committee for military affairs. Every agency, every business, every locality was organized. The schools, the churches, the Aid Societies, the Boards, each and every one labored for those who were leaving home, or for those left at home. Committees of citizens worked in every neighborhood to help those who were ignorant of the procedure, and to whom the questionnaire was more mysterious than the blank form of a personal tax report.

At many a house in the County, where there was a man or woman who had an education or wrote a good hand, groups of young men would be seen awaiting the much needed assistance so readily furnished, and discussing among themselves the future which seemed so full of mystery.

The Court House was the center of activity. From it came the mysterious postal card announcing the class of the young soldiers, and fixing the time at which the new recruits were to assemble there to take their departure for the life of the camp.

Then the spirit of the county was seen in its fulness. Committees of men and women appeared to receive the young men and generally, in the school auditorium or in the Court room, addresses were made, refreshments served, and other forms of entertainment indulged in.

Serious as was the business which called these meetings, it was rare indeed that anything was allowed which might sadden or depress those leaving home. Those meetings were ever the most notably gay and festive that the boys had ever attended. Jokes, songs, and merry laughter characterized them, and it was only on the following morning when the band of youngsters took the train for Camp Lee or other camps that there was sometimes seen the element of sadness incident to such leave-taking. Even that situation was relieved by the attention of the good women with coffee and other refreshments for their young neighbors and friends.

As the soldiers left for their posts of duty, those left behind set about organizing the elements that made for efficiency in helping the soldier abroad and his family at home.

A new impetus was given to the Boy Scout movement. There were two or more troops in the County, whose active participation in meetings held for the benefit of the soldiers was as noticeable as was their service in

COLONEL WILLIAM NELSON.

the sale of bonds and Savings Stamps valuable. The neighborhoods were laid off into sections and every family visited and given an opportunity to subscribe.

The Hanover Bank was the first bank to raise its quota in one of the Liberty Loan "Drives."

Subscriptions were cheerfully made, and there was a generous rivalry among the youngsters as they proclaimed with eloquence the needs of the soldier and his family, and the duty of those who did not have to go to war to maintain those who went, and those bereft by their going.

In at least one Hanover family, there is now the highly prized bronze medal sent one of the boys for services rendered the country in the sale of Government bonds in the neighborhood of the boy's home.

The work of the Red Cross and of the other Societies in the County has been already referred to. Every known means was resorted to by them. Each school in the County was visited, and the children urged to buy Savings Stamps. These visits were very successful.

Two County Meetings

A typical meeting held at the Aaron Hall School, in the upper end of the County, may be described. Major C. Cotesworth Pinckney, in charge of the Red Cross Work at Lee Camp, was appealed to, and sent to the meeting a notable trio—Kal Johnson, Dr. Slattery, and Chaplain Robert Nelson. A great crowd was assembled. The Parish minister opened the meeting with prayer; the Boy Scouts went through their manual of exercises, among other things "wig-wagging" messages; the speakers told eloquently of the needs of the men going over seas, and of the work of the organizations. The climax was reached, however, when an old Confederate Soldier, William Elisha Harris, spoke in simple, but eloquent language, and exhorted all present to realize what was expected of all good citizens—young and old. He concluded by an appeal to the memory of those who had themselves given their lives to the Cause they held sacred.

Before Armistice Day, the most notable day in the period of the World War was the 19th day of April, 1918. It was proclaimed throughout the County as "Liberty Day," and the whole County notified to appear at Ashland. Perhaps more credit was due to the efforts of the late Parkin Scott, Esquire, who was the manager and treasurer of the Liberty Day Exercises, than to any other person. Though where all did so much any special mention may appear invidious.

William P. Shelton, a Confederate Veteran, was Marshal, with two other veterans, Sam E. Baker and William Blunt, as Aides. There were Reception Committees of the leading men and women of the County, headed by the Mayor of Ashland, the Hon. Andrew Ellis, with Judge Richard H. Cardwell, Mr. George P. Haw, and Mr. Rosewell Page as members. The Ladies' Reception Committee were Mrs. Charles P. Cardwell, Mrs. C. P. Blakey, Mrs. W. P. Shelton, and Mrs. Deitrick. The Committee on Singing and Music had as Manager, Mrs. J. C. Blasingame; that on Vaudeville, Mr. Webb Midyette, as manager; that on the Red Cross had Mrs. Henry R. Carter.

In the parade were "the War Brides, Mothers, Wives, Sisters and Sweethearts of our Heroes, wearing a Service Flag." There were the Hanover Grays, under Commander Floyd Tucker; the students of Randolph-Macon College, under Commander Munce; the Boy Scouts, under Chief Scout Weaver; the Junior Boy Scouts, under Commander Dugdale. Then came the Committees of the Town Council, the Judge and Board of Supervisors. Then came School Children and the Colored Societies.

After a formal parade, the Mayor introduced the Hon. Henry T. Wickham, who presided. Prayer was offered by Bishop D. J. O'Connell, of Richmond. After music, the presiding officer introduced United States Senator Claude A. Swanson, the orator of the occasion, who made a noble address.

At the close of the day, it was thought by all present to have been, perhaps, the most notable celebration ever held in the County.

The music was "America," "The Star-Spangled Banner," "Onward Christian Soldiers," and "Over There," with with the Chorus:

> "Send the word over there
> That the Yanks are coming,
> The drums rum-tumming everywhere.
> So prepare, say a prayer,
> Send the word, beware;
> We'll be over, we're coming over
> Over there; over there!"

and "Keep the Home Fires Burning."

Those from the County who gave their lives for the cause of Liberty were:

Leslie A. Dodge, William Duke, William E. Harper, Clarence Buckner, Gus Mills, A. M. Porter, Edwin T. Jenkns, Otway Tribble, Dr. E. L. Goodwin, and Lawrence J. Melton. Their names and memories are still cherished by their neighbors and friends.

The mortality among our soldiers, considering the epidemic of Influenza that raged, was not surprisingly great.

The Home Guard Company organized in Ashland has been referred to. It was duly enrolled as a State Volunteer Company, and inspected by General Jo Lane Stern.

At Randolph-Macon College there was a fine company of young men known as the S. A. T. C. (the Students Army Training Corps). A stranger might well have mistaken the campus for that of a Military Institution.

Besides those already mentioned, Hanover had Rear Admiral Hilary P. Jones, Lieutenant-Commander W. C. Wickham, Captain Charles T. Johnson, Major Richard F. Beirne, of the Artillery; Captain Henry R. Carter, Captain Stuart C. Leake, Major Herbert C. Mallory, and Lieutenant William D. Cardwell.

In the list of "Distinguished Service" have been mentioned Melville Hunter Dunn, Gordon Hammond, Carl James Strause, and William P. Tignor.

No account of Hanover's war activities is complete without a tribute to the women who, while their County men went to the front, and their sisters worked at home, went themselves, and encountered at Seven Pines, Penniman, and elsewhere, the dangers of the explosives used in making shells and weighing powder, driving trucks, and making the Motor Corps of young women as notable as any branch of the service.

There were instances of Hanover women who did these things. When a letter was received inquiring about the risk of the Seven Pines Powder Loading Plant to those engaged, a Hanover man, whose daughter was thus engaged, replied that "any woman who spent the working hours weighing or packing gunpowder was risking her life for the sake of her country."

World War Soldiers and Sailors.

A

Anderson, L. B.
Almond, Earnest K.
Ancell, Vincent C., Jr.
Andrews, R. L.
Arnold, A. L.
Abrams, W.
Adams, J.
Allen, J.
Allen, E. L.
Atkinson, B. J.
Anderson, J. L.
Atkins, L. T.
Anderson C.
Anderson, R.
Albert, R.

B

Bowles, G. H.
Baldwin, F. V., Jr.
Breeden, Byrd.
Beirne, Major Rich. F.
Beirne, Lieut. Frank F.
Burruss, Grant
Buchanan, Wm. Edw.
Bagby, Simon
Burruss, Grayson L.
Brown, Lin.
Brown, Walter
Bowles, John H.
Bradley, F. B.
Broaddus, C. C.
Buchanan, L . A.
Brown, S. J.
Brown, J. M.
Brooks, S. W.
Brooks, C. R.
Bush, A.
Bush, M.
Brooks, O. J.
Brooks, Harry.
Baylor, Corbin
Brown, John Mills
Bowles, Thos. Stanley
Brown, Claude McLane
Butler, Fred A.
Bartlett, Junius, Jr.
Bazile, Leon Maurice Nelson
Bullock, Arthur R.

Baker, B. F.
Brokenbrough, W. J.
Bosher, A. A.
Bosher, E. G.
Brooks, I.
Brooks, A. O.
Butler, J. L.
Brooks, J. R.
Buckner, C.
Bradley, L. A.
Brooks, C. F.
Braxton, F.
Braxton, B.
Butler, H.
Bowles, M. R.
Baylor, H.
Blincoe, J. W.
Brooks, H. G.

C

Cardwell, Lieut.-Com. Wm. D.
Cardwell, W. H.
Carpenter, J. F.
Cephas, M.
Carrington, Gratton
Cardwell, Richard H.
Carter, John
Carter, Capt. Henry R.
Carter, Asst. Sur. Genl. Henry R.
Cooke, Chas. B. Jr.
Campbell, Capt. Carroll V.
Chenery, Asst. Sur. Jean J.
Chenery, Capt. Christopher T.
Cauthorne, Chas. Edw.
Crowe, Jas. Otho
Cash, T.
Cash, J. D.
Cash, Richard
Crawford, C. T.
Carter, Saml. Bayon
Christian, Geo. W.
Chamberlain, G.
Christopher, James W.
Crump, Royal Alex. B.
Christian, Emanuel
Chandler, Bennie
Coleman, Parke
Cauthorne, Wilton Howard
Cannon, Robt. L.

Carter, Joseph
Carter, J. W.
Childress, Robt. Edw.
Clory, Alex H.
Cosby, Robt.
Clew, Lonnie
Cypress, John Burton
Claytor, R.
Clarke, E. T.
Carter. W.
Carlton, J. C.
Clarke, A. T.
Crouch, W. L.
Clements, G. S.
Clayton, Sam
Colavita, M. J.
Crump, R. A. B.
Coates, W. C.

D

Crenshaw, E.
Dent, H. O.
Dugdale. Jos. H.
Dunn, Hunter
Deitrick, Lieut. S. C., Jr.
Dickenson, Thomas
Dodge, Leslie A.
Dodge, Howard E.
Duke, Lieut. Thos. L.
Duke, L. A.
Duggins, Onley Colston
Durvin, Harry Jefferson
Detwiler, Clarence H.
Deals, G. W.
Deals, Eugene Washington
Dabney, Thos. Lewis
Dabney, Rich. Leslie
Dabney, McClellan
Dulling. Philip Other
Davis, Franklin
Davis, Sam
Davis, Cosie Moore
Davis, W.
Dandridge, Hartwell A.
Dickerson, T.
Delarue, E. G.
Dosett, J. E.
Davis, J. W.
Dunn, W. L.
Duke, A. M.
Duke, W. L.

Dabney, M. M.
DeJarnette, J. C.

E

DeJarnette, J. C., Jr.
Evans, Corp. Wm. E.
Ellis, A. J.
Ellis, F. S.
Elllis, Charles
Ellett, Harry Ashton
Edwards, C. W.
Ellis, J. G.

F

Fleet, Rutherfoord
Fountain, Daniel
Flannigan, Chas. Ballard
Frick, Arthur.
Fox, F. M., Jr.
Fox, H. C.
Fountain, C.
Fountain, E. W.
Ferrell, H.
Foster, J.
Fleet, A. R.

G

Goodwin, Lieut. Edw. L.
Gilman, John Gilford
Golden, Thurmond
Green, John Wesley
Green, Lewis
Garrett, Bernard Cullen
Golden, Thermon
Glass, H. M.
Gray, Andrew
Gallimore, Henry
Gaines, Aubrey
Gaines, D.
Gordon, Oscar .
Gatewood, J. B.
Gammon, M.
Garrett, W. P.
Gouldin, A. B.
Green, J. E.
Givins, H. B.

H

Harrold, Herbert
Hammond, Gordon
Hammond, William A., Jr.
Hart, Macon
Harris, W. T.
Huffman, F. B.

Haden, Clifton
Haden, Samuel
Henderson, B.
Howison, M. L.
Houston, W. A.
Hardgrove, J.
Harris, C. O.
Hughes, Frank L.
Hootman, Perry
Harper, Wm. E.
Harris, Allen Montgomery
Hayes, H. L.
Hall, C. J.
Hall, Chas. Henry
Harlow, J. R.
Harper, G. T.
Hubbard, Wilbet
Hewlett, John Milton
Hall, Chas. Lin.
Hughes, Eugene P.
Howard, Edward
Hopkins, T. C.
Hart, H. G.
Hall, A. K.
Harris, S.
Hunter, P. R.
Hutcheson, H. E.
Holmes, K. A.
Hill, F. H.
Henderson, A.
Hughes, S. H.
Harris, J. F.
Harlow, A. S.
Hatcher, S. P.
Higgason, W. T.
Henley, W.
Hunt, G. J.
Howison, J. F., Jr.
Hunt, A. L., Jr.

I

Iverson, Americus
Imobersteg, H. D.
Iverson, Jefferson

J

Jones, Rear Admiral Hilary P.
Jones, Wm. C.
Johnson, Capt. Chas. F.
Jenkins, Luther
Jenkins, C. H.
James, Geo.

Jones, J.
Jones, Edw.
Jones, Edw. P.
Jenkins, Ed. Thos.
Johnson, Arthur.
Jones, Irvin
James, Geo. Wise
Johnson, John A.
Jones, Cornelius, Jr.,
Jordan, Dr. J. Wood.
Jones, C., Jr.
Jackson, Philip.
Jackson, Wm. Clarence
Jackson, Andrew
Jackson, W.
Jones, James
Jackson, Benj. J.
Jinkins, J. M.
Jackson, J. L.
Jones, Richard
Johnson, H.
James, R. L.
James, Phil.
Jones, C. B.
Jenkins, R.
Jackson, J.

K

King, H.
King, G.
Kerr, Drury D.
Kersey, L. W.
Kimbrough, Lewis T.
Kimbrough, A. P.
King, W.
Kersey, J. W.
Kannon, M. M.
Kersey, K. K.
Kersey, H.

L

Lucas, Asst. Eng. Harry.
Leake, Capt. Stuart C.
Lancaster, Chaplain Rich.
Lee, Clifton, Jr.
Lane, Edw. Lewis
Lloyd, F. V.
Lightfoot, I.
Lane, R. T.
Lucas, J. V.
Lane, P. W.
Lucas, Chas. T.

Lane, Harry Scott
Lancaster, G. Douglas
Lowry, Linwood.
Leake, M. R.
Luck, C. S., Jr.
Luck, Thos. Stuart
Luck, Earnest J.
Luck, Chas. Merle
Lawrence, Wm.
Lee, Rev. Wm. B., Jr.
Lumpkin, C. S.
Landrum, W. W.
Landrum, E. F.
Lucas, Thos. E.
Lewis, L.
Lipscomb, C.

M

Moss, C. W.
Mosby, Ben
Martin, R. F.
Martin, L. H.
Mason, Robt.
Mosby, G. C.
Midyette, Lieut. D. R., Jr.
Mallory, Major Herbert C.
Martin, R. L.
Mickins, W.
Marye, Lieut. Robt. Waller
Mason, Herbert Thos.
Moss, Thos. Overton, Ensign
Mills, Nickols
Mills, Clarence
Moore, Arthur.
Mills, Gus Wade
Martin, John Lewis
Monroe, Geo. Lee
Melton, Guy
Mallory, I. A.
Marshall, C.
Moore, W. H.
Morris, W. B.
Morris, E. M.
Madison, E. P.
Meyberg, S. K.
Miller, E.
Mines, W. T.
Midyette, W. B.
Midyette, J. W.
Martin, R. F.
Miller, G. M.
Moody, S. M.

Mills, B. H.
Mallory, W. N.
Mickens, J.
Melton, L. J.
McGhee, T. H.
Miller, I. L.
Marshall, J.
Matthews, M. L.
Monday, A.
Morris, C. H.
Morris, L. G.
Mickens, W.
Meyberg, L. O.
Mayo, Jno. H.

N

Nolley, Lieut. Henry C.
Nuchols, Wm. D.
Napper, Garfield
Noel, S. T.

O

Oliver, C. H.
Oliver, Stuart A.
Owens, Raymond Bruce
Oliver, A. L.

P

Puller, Chas. H.
Price, Daniel
Price, A. F.
Perrin, Sergt. P. P.
Postans, W.
Postans, R.
Porter, Amos
Prosser, Lieut. Fred K.
Powell, Conway
Payne, Claude C.
Potts, Lieut. Jos. Johnson
Parkinson, Lieut. Jos. Wm.
Priddy, Wm. Vaughan
Puller, Henry Golden
Perry, Marion Reid
Perrin, Ollie Jas.
Parrish, E.
Parrish, Carroll M.
Peregoy, Chas. B.
Poteat, Samuel
Poteat, Silvester
Price, Moses, Jr.
Parsley, Herbert
Perkins, Willard C.
Price, Daniel Howard

Pettis, John
Patterson, John
Perkins, J. W.
Parkinson, W. C., Jr.
Pierce, J. M.
Priddy, N.
Priddy, J. B.
Page, J. I.
Parsley, L. A.
Parsley, L. M.
Perrin, S. W.

Q

Quarles, Frank
Quarles, Oliver
Quarles, Levi
Quarles, C.

R

Redd, Champe
Rice, Leyle
Rice, Corp. Borden P.
Rice, Geo. Henry
Rice, Edward
Rice, B. P.
Robinson, Richard
Robertson, W.
Robertson, Willie
Robinson, Wilson
Robinson, Roscoe
Richardson, Venable
Radford, Wm. Cardwell
Roane, A.
Robinson, Ellis A.
Romaine, L. C.
Robertson, J. G.
Roberts, J. M.

S

Stebbins (Mate), Chas.
Spreati, Peter
Stanley, Walter
Shipley, Wilbur
Shelton, J.
Shepherd, Major
Smith, Henry
Stone, H. G.
Stone, W. A.
Stone, Jas. Minor, Jr.
Stewart, Cutley Edward
Shelton, Richard
Shelton, S. W.
Seger, Thos.
Southward, H. L.

Shortell, Frank James
Strause, Americus N.
Stiefbold, John Fred
Satterwhite, C. F.
Satterwhite, Lonnie Thos.
Satterwhite, V. W.
Starke, Robert Walker
Scott, Wm. Henry
Stone, Ollie Clements
Swink, Jasper
Stiefbold, H. J.
Smith, P.
Smith, T. J.
Skidmore, E. C.
Stanley, W. T.
Stanley, C. A.
Stanley, H.
Stanley, W. G.
Strause, T.
Satterwhite, E. E.
Sale, J. I.
Shelton, L.
Simpson, J.
Stanley, E. E.
Stanley, G. A.
Starke, G. A.
Shelton, G.
Stone, A. P.
Samuel, J. B.
Skillman, W. O.
Stone, B. O.
Spicer, C. A.
Smithers, Thos. John
Stebbins, Harvey R.
Simmonds, Sidney G.
Sydnor, Walter, Jr.

T

Temple, Frank.
Taylor (Nurse), Martha Elizabeth
Trevillian, Thos. B.
Tyler, Asst. Surg. Geo. Boyd
Thurston, Jesse Saml.
Taylor, Dalton
Taylor, Philip Lynn
Taylor, Abraham L.
Taliaferro, Wilmer Russell
Taliaferro, J.
Tyler, Wm.
Tyler, H. C.
Terrell, Frank Martin

Tignor, Wm. Prosser
Tignor, H. G.
Timberlake, John Cabell
Tribble, Otway Thos.
Tunstall, Theo. Arthur
Terrell, James Floyd
Terrell, Phillip
Terrell, Wm. S.
Tate, Jos. Woodie
Tyler, Haley
Tunstall, Frank
Taylor, John
Taylor, Joe
Tyler, J. P.
Tyson, Jas. Allen
Thompson, Jos. Linwood
Taylor, Buford Tucker
Thompson, Edgar Harrold
Tinsley, M.
Thaniel, W. A.
Thomas, Rich. Stanley
Thompson, Harold
Tuck, W. J.
Thompson, W. A.
Thornton, W. L.
Talley, J. W.
Tate, R. E.
Talley, O. L.
Thompson, R. L.
Thomas, E.
Thurston, W. R.
Taylor, R.
Tyree, T.
Tener, G. R.
Tuck, E. A.
Tignor, J. M.
Thompson, V. H.
Thompson, D.
Turner, E. B.
Timberlake, G. M.
Terrell, R. L.
Thomas, Stuart
Talley, C. C.
Tate, J. C.
Thaniel, T. E.
Thaniel, A.
Thomas, J. P.
Trainum, M. A.
Tucker, A. C., Jr.
Timberlake, B. E.

U

Updike, I. A.
Updike, G. Z.

V

Vial, P. M.
Vass, E. S.
Vaughan, William Walton
Vaughan, C. E.

W

Woodfin, Solon Boston
Woodfin, Clifton B., Jr.
Woodfin, Thos. N.
Waldrop, Bertran M.
West, C. A.
Wilson, W. A.
Wickham, Wms. C., Lieut. Com.
Wickham, Geo. B.
Wightman, Lieut. Eugene J.
Wightman, Yeoman John Thos.
White, Edgar
Winston, Oliver J.
Weisinger, Wm. G.
Wiltgen, E. M.
Wiltgen, Wm. Alois
Wright, Wm. Earnest
Wright, Louis
Wright, Adele
Williams, Timothy
Willie, V. P.
Walker, Howard
Williams, Junius
Waldrop, T. W. B.
Wingfield, Lewis Ellis
Waters, Willie A.
Wood, Cecil Gilmar
Walton, Ashby Vernon
Winston, Sherman B.
Willis, Wm. Horace
Woolfolk, Hilton Robt.
Williams, Wm. L.
Woolfolk, L. E.
Woolfolk, K. C.
Woody, H.
White, F.
Williams, R.
Washington, J.
Winston, S.
White, Geo.
Woodson, J. H.
Woodson, G. F.

Watkins, W.
Wickham, J. B.
Woody, T.
Wright, J. L.
Woodfin, W. C.

Wright, W. B.
Wood, L. N.

Y

Yarborough, H. F.

The Hanover branch of the War History Commission was J. Walton Hall, chairman; Miss Mary Wilkie, and George E. Haw.

Rosewell Page of Hanover, as Second Auditor of Virginia, was ex-officio a member of the State Council of Defense.

PERSONAL NOTES

Hanover, though largely an agricultural section, and the lower end adapted to the culture of vegetables and melons, as mentioned, gives constantly to the population of Richmond and to the personnel of the railroads that traverse her borders, a considerable percentage of her people.

The introduction of automobiles, telephones, and electric lights, and the establishment of good roads in all directions through the County have done much to add to the comfort and convenience of the people, and are doing much toward making permanent the settlement of our citizens.

Several years ago, there came to the upper end of the County a Bohemian settlement that undertook to observe some community idea which had worked in the old country whence they came. It was soon found, however, that there were too many opportunities for individual effort, and so little need for such a combination that the community idea was abandoned, and the customs of this country adopted. There are still in Hanover a number of these good citizens, who by their thrift and industry have added to the wealth of the County.

Hanover has had a notable record in its citizenship. Reference has been made to notables of the last century. Perhaps after Patrick Henry, the most notable speaker the County has produced was Richard Morris, whose descendants still own "Taylor's Creek." A specimen of his eloquence may be seen in the report of the Constitutional Convention of 1829-30, and evidence of the charm of his voice in Governor Wise's description of it as the "vox argentia."

The story of the effect of Mr. Morris' argument may be gathered from the action of John Randolph, of Roanoke, who after the speech made upon the question of slave representation, came up to the orator and exclaimed, "Sir, I preceive that, as of old, wise men still come from the East." His sons, Edward W. Morris and Charles Morris, inherited much of their father's eloquence, and it seems to have been passed on to the present generation, as there are few finer speakers than the Rev. James Morris, grandson of Mr. Richard Morris, now a missionary in Brazil.

The Rev. Patrick Henry was for forty years rector of St. Paul's Parish. The Rev John Cooke was for many years rector of St. Martin's. Among churchmen, natives of Hanover, may be mentioned the Rev. Doctor Robert Nelson, who was for thirty years a missionary in China, and the Rev. John Dabney, missionary to Brazil, and the Rev. Dr. Frank Page, who died as rector of Truro Parish, Fairfax County, Virginia. The Rev. S. S. Hepburn was for two generations a notable pastor in Hanover, as was Dr. Ryland for many years. Among the great preachers who have been heard in the County have been Dr. Duncan Dr. Bitting, Dr. Burroughs, and Dr. Granberry, and Samuel Davies, already mentioned.

Among doctors, in the early days, Dr. Honeyman was perhaps the best known. His name now survives in the bridge over Little River, near Trinity Church. The celebrated Dr. James McClurg was also a practitioner in Hanover, and there is a field there called within the memory of living men "McClurg's Old Field." The Wickhams, in the upper end of Hanover, are his descendants. Doctor Carter Berkeley, of Edgewood, was famous in his day. There have been three generations of notable doctors in the Anderson family—the last of whom, Dr. Herman Anderson, died recently, greatly lamented.

In the lower end of the County have been in past years, Dr. Henry Curtis, Dr. Wat H. Tyler, of "Tarwood," brother of President Tyler; Dr. William Macon, of Ingleside; Dr. Charles R. Cullen, and Dr. Talley, who had six sons in the Confederate army. There were also Dr. Fox, Dr. Meredith, Dr. Hope, Dr. Woolridge, Dr. Charles E. Thompson, Dr. Cawthorne, Dr. Goodall, Dr. Gregory, Dr. Scott, Dr. Winston, Dr. Fleming, and his son, Dr. George W. Fleming; Dr. Brackett, Dr. Hatch, and Dr. Charles James Terrell, who has recently died at a great age.

Not to mention others who now so well represent the medical faculty, Dr. Henry Rose Carter was the most distinguished of the County's physicians. As co-laborers with Gorgas and Walter Reed, he became famous as a great Sanitarian, and reflected credit upon his County and country.

In science, the County has had the geologist, William M. Fontaine; in literature and statesmanship. Thomas Nelson Page; and in scholarship, Major John Page, William F. Wickham, Henry T. Wickham and Alfred Duke, Esquires, and those who taught in the schools mentioned, and those scholars who teach at Randolph-Macon College, where once taught Thomas R. Price, the great scholar, whose people went from the neighborhood of the Fork Church.

Hanover's soldiers were headed in rank by General Williams C. Wickham. Colonel Lewis Minor Coleman, and Captain Dabney Harrison lost their lives in battle, as did many other gallant citizens as already recounted. The venerable George P. Haw, so long Commonwealth's attorney of the County, lost his arm at Sharpsburg. No officers of equal rank were more fortunate in their commands or more notable in their rank than the Hanover Artillery Colonels—Hilary P. Jones, William Nelson, and Lewis M. Coleman.

Hanover has the unique history of having had father and son speakers of the House of Delegates in the case of the Hon. Richard H. Cardwell, and the Hon. Wm. D. Cardwell, and State Senators in the case of General Wms. C. Wickham and the Hon. Henry T. Wickham.

COUNTY GOVERNMENT AND BAR.

Hanover has generally been fortunate in its County Government. After the War between the States there was some confusion, and there were some indifferent men in control; but her good citizens soon came again into control of the County's affairs.

The old County Court System, when the Magistrates of the several Districts came together at the Court House and sat as a Court, was very satisfactory and the best men in the County were found upon the Bench.

The presiding Justice was ex-officio sheriff, and the duties now performed by the Treasurer of the County were then performed by the sheriff in addition to the other duties of his office. George W. Doswell was Treasurer of the County for a longer period, perhaps, than any other citizen in its history. For many years General Williams C. Wickham served as a member of the Board of Supervisors, though at that time the head of the Chesapeake and Ohio Railroad.

The Clerkship has in recent years been held by the Taylor family, whose efficiency has made them the typically useful members of the County's official society. One of the interesting things connected with the history of the County is that three notable families in the County have held the Clerkship of the County almost continuously since its formation—the Pollards, Winstons, and Taylors. Among the notable men who have started their career in the Clerk's office may be mentioned Judge Edmund Waddill, Jr., of the United States Court; as did Henry Clay, who it will be remembered wrote in Mr. Tinsley's office then Clerk of the Court in Richmond, where he made the acquaintance of

THOS. NELSON PAGE.

Chancellor Wythe, to whom he was so much indebted as he himself declared.

Charles Chiswell, Clerk of the General Court, lived in Hanover, where he died in April, 1737. His son, Col. John Chiswell, who represented the County as Burgess from 1745 to 1755, killed Robert Routledge, a Scotchman, in an altercation in the old tavern at Hanover Court House in 1766.

Hanover County has been fortunate in its Judiciary. At one time John Henry, father of Patrick Henry, was the presiding justice, as was later Francis Page, the father of Major John Page.

Judge John White Brockenbrough, the distinguished judge and law teacher at Washington College, was born in Hanover on the 10th of July, 1778. Among distinguished men born in Hanover, who lived elsewhere, was General Thomas Sumpter (now Sumter), of South Carolina, who, according to the family Bible, was born here August 14, 1734. (Letter of A. S. Salley, Jr., Hist. Com. of S. C.) It will be recalled as a coincidence that when Fort Sumter was fired on in 1861, the first shot was fired by Edmund Ruffin, then a citizen of Hanover. Thus was the County represented in the names of two notable citizens in the naming and in the overthrow of the fort which some have thought the beginning of the War between the States.

Judge Samuel C. Redd was for more than a generation the County Judge, as was Judge Newman for a short time, and in the Circuit Court, Judge William S. Barton presided long enough to see a second generation of lawyers at the Hanover Bar.

The abolishing of the County Courts in 1902 has been thought of doubtful policy, as the County Judge was enabled to become familiar with the needs of the County in a way that one who lives outside can only learn after long experience. This is especially true in the matter of police regulation, where an intimate knowledge of the local conditions is so necessary for its proper administration.

Of the idea that the new system is more economical, it may be said that the matter is at least doubtful, as the Circuit Judges now have to spend much time in trying cases which would naturally fall to the County Judge, with his intimate knowledge of local conditions and local relations, and prisoners often have to await the meetings of the Circuit Court, which meets every other month instead of every month, as the County Court did.

The following is a list of "the Gentlemen Justices" of the Peace in Hanover for the years 1764, 1767, and 1770:

John Henry
Richard Johnson
John Snelson
Essex William Winston
Wm. Taylor
James Littlepage
Nathaniel West Dandridge
John Sims
John Syme
John Boswell
William Thompson
Nelson Berkeley
Francis Smith
Charles Goodall
Samuel Meredith

Charles Smith
Thomas Garland
John Webb
Garland Anderson
John Webb
Anthony Winston (Sheriff)
Samuel Overton
Samuel Gist
Henry Gilbert
John Meriwether (Quo)
William Macon, Jr. (Quo)
Peter Fountain
Meriwether Skelton
John Starke (Quo)
Charles Crenshaw

William Morris

Geddes Winston

John Gilbert

Peter Fontaine

Benjamin Anderson

John Smith

John Lawrence

John Robinson

The lists published in the Bulletin of the Virginia State Library give an admirable idea of the high standing of the Courts of that period. The names listed as Justices from the various counties are the best known in the history of the Commonwealth. Those men were well worthy of the encomium passed upon them by Chief Justice Marshall in the Convention of 1829-30.

Our modern Justices of the Peace are still chosen from our good citizens.

Hanover has always been noted for its able Bar. That Bar has been supplemented by some of the best lawyers of Richmond and the adjacent counties. Of these may be mentioned James Lyons, the Stanards, John Minor Botts, John L. Marye, Marmaduke Johnson, John A. Meredith, John B. Young, John Howard, William W. Crump, The Holladays, Edmund Waddill, Jr., Cabell, Christian, Sands, and Mr. Griswold. From other counties came Aylett, Leake, Gordon, and Gregory.

Hanover's Commonwealth Attorneys in recent years have been Geo. Wm. Richardson, John Page, Hill Carter, Geo. P. Haw, Walter Sydnor, and Andrew J. Ellis. Geo. P. Haw held the position for more than a generation. There have been few better prosecutors; and the criminal laws have always been duly enforced to the satisfaction of the people.

Judge Richard H. Cardwell, until his resignation, was on the Court of Appeals, and won a high place in the opinion of all who know his work. Judge Edmund Waddill, was a regular practioner at the Hanover Bar when he was elevated to the Federal Bench. His high standing is a matter of pride to all the citizens of Hanover.

Major John Page was, in point of service, at the time of his death, the oldest member of the Hanover Bar. He possessed a fine scholarship and brilliant wit, which made him interesting as an advocate and charming as a speaker.

Edward Watts Morris was an eloquent speaker, and one of the most brilliant talkers of his time. He was the last of the conversationalists, who, in any company, attracted all present to listen.

Hill Carter was the leader of the Hanover Bar at the time of his death, as he was perhaps of the State Bar. Apart from his other gifts, his forte lay in the strength and humor with which his argument and conversation alike were crowded. His manners in court were the best, and his arguments models of close reasoning and lucid illustration.

William Josiah Leake was a great Chancery lawyer, as is Addison Holladay, both of whom occupied judicial positions in Richmond.

Chastain White and William R. Winn were notable lawyers of the County in their time. Willoughby Newton died comparatively a young man, and left behind the reputation of an industrious, honorable, and successful career.

Henry T. Wickham has long enjoyed the reputation of being a great corporation lawyer. He has devoted his notable professional career mainly to that branch of the profession.

Walter Sydnor has maintained the high character of the Hanover Bar, and has enjoyed a good practice. Thomas Nelson Page was a regular practioner at the

Hanover Bar until his literary work overshadowed his fine gifts as a lawyer.

The present Bar has its quota of good lawyers who are maintaining the high standards described in the older men mentioned.

Until the days of automobiles it was the custom of the Bar in attendance on the Courts in Hanover to stay at the Court House until the Court adjourned. Many of the lawyers rode to Court on horseback. Often two or more would be sleeping in the same room, and their meetings after the day's labors were over, in the Judge's room, or elsewhere, were famous for good stories and witty sallies, which made the younger members of the Bar at home with their elder brethren.

The flood gates of anecdote and reminiscence would be opened by some senior addressing a young lawyer and asking, "Did you ever hear the story of how Hill Carter escaped being hanged for horse stealing by having the plea of idiocy put in for him?" Then that gentleman would have to tell of his being sent by the new Captain of the Caroline Troop to catch his horse, and how he had caught one he thought the Captain's, when he was met by a squad who were out looking for a horse thief, who had stolen several horses, and how they said they would hang him, when fortunately Norval Harris saw him and acquitted him by saying: "Let that boy go! That's Hill Carter. He hasn't got real good sense anyhow! He aint more than half witted!"

CHARACTERISTICS

Hanover County has had many interesting personages, and some of unusual cleverness. Many stories are still remembered and re-told in social gatherings.

Colonel Perrin's reply to Mr. Lyons' too personal cross-examination was, "Some people take Mr. Jimmie Lyons for a public orator; but as for me, I have followed him for forty years and have never overtaken him in a single proposition. I have always found him dull, prolix, periphrastic, and ambagatory."

Mr. Henry Doswell's reply to the orator inveighing against the public school and declaring that his education had never cost his father but twelve dollars was, "Yes; and Sir, your father never got the worth of his money!"

A Hanover citizen replied overwhelmingly to the assistant prosecutor who had asked what the brand of liquor was which he was charged with dispensing without a license, "Well, Sir; it was the same brand that I sold you three gallons of when you ran against Captain Wickham for the Senate and for which you have never paid me yet."

When an irate gentleman asked Major Page if he had said so and so, he replied, "Well, I don't remember whether I ever said it, but I'll say so now!" He also made the humorous reply to the question why he felt so bitterly towards some Mormons who had come to the County: "I can't afford to let two of my neighbors be confirmed in the theory of Mormonism, who have lived in the practice of it all their lives!"

When the litigant who had brought an action was asked it he had counsel and he replied "the Justice said he'd be my counsel," Major Page replied, to the amusement of the bystanders, "You've chosen the best!"

Judge Cardwell, when asked by the President of the Court how many opinions he had for that morning, replied: "I am like Dyson's little boy who was out hare hunting yesterday. When I asked him how many hares he had, he said, 'When I get this one I'm after and one more I'll have two!'"

When Colonel Beirne was in the upper end of Hanover to escape arrest prior to the meeting with Colonel Elam, his friends took him to an old homestead then unoccupied, and one of them, who was something of a musician, entertained the gentleman about to appear on the "field of Honor" by picking out on the old piano "The Dead March in 'Saul!'"

When a Militia general, then recently appointed, demanded of a bystander who the gentleman was that passed and was told that it was Colonel Hilary Jones, one of General Lee's famous artillerymen, the offended general said: "The —— fellow had the insolence to call me Captain just now as I passed him!"

When Mr. Hill Carter and Major Page represented a citizen of Louisa upon a charge of larceny in the Hustings Court of Richmond, and put a witness on the stand who the client said would prove his good character, he was asked how long he had known the accused and what was his reputation in his community for good character. The witness answered that, man and boy, he had known him for nigh sixty years; that enduring the war he was taken up for stealing a sheep, and once since the war he was taken up for stealing tobacco, and that "with them two exceptions, his character was as good as anybody's in the County!"

During the war, the conscript guard came into the upper end of the County to arrest some who were "absent from duty without leave." Miss Sally, whose brother was sought, met the soldiers at the door as the brother took to the bush out of the back window. She greeted the soldiers pleasantly and reported her brother as having left home. Then she delivered herself as follows: "Gentlemen, William ain't no warrior. He wasn't cut out for Mr. Jeff Davis' war. I jes wish I could fight in the army! But I can't; though I do think every man is the best judge of his own spunk!"

When General Joseph E. Johnson, a candidate for Congress, was asked by an influential citizen on the Hanover Court Green to go to dinner with him as the Tavern bell rang and the General politely declined, saying he did not dine until seven o'clock, it took some time to appease the influential citizen, who protested that he "didn't see how he could vote for a man who didn't know the difference between dinner and supper!"

MUSTERS, ETC.

Before the Civil War there were regular Musters held at the Court House, and Muster Day was the event of the month. The parade ground was in the field back of the Tavern, and, as now, there was then a deep gorge or moraine near the edge, grown up in bushes and briars, which was indeed a tangled thicket.

In the course of the exercises one of the companies present, in making its evolutions obedient to the orders of its Captain, who was quite ignorant of the proper command, advanced into the gorge and got into inextricable confusion, to the amusement of the other companies and of the crowd of spectators.

The Colonel, in all the majesty of cocked hat, full regimentals, and drawn sword, galloped to the rescue, and called out in stentorian tones: "Captain; what in the —— are you a-doin' in them thar bushes? Git your company out thar and form!"

The Captain thus addressed, as cool as the Colonel was hot, responded in a voice to be heard all over the parade ground that he knew of "no command for a revolution of that kind."

Under a shower of oaths from the Colonel, and amid the laughter of the other companies, the Captain finally extricated his company, but with commands which none but he had ever heard before, and which none has ever heard since: "On the North flank, Gee! Git up Center! Haw, South flank! Out to the opening! March!"

At another Muster, the aforesaid Captain claimed as the senior officer, in the absence of the Major, the right to parade on horseback. He received the following rebuff from the Colonel, who remembered the Captain's confused orders on the previous meeting: "You aint gwine to parade on no horse here today, Captain."

A distinguished citizen of the County has left an interesting account of one of these meetings. How on a broiling-hot day the Colonel with his staff, all in gala attire, waited in vain for the review which was to take place by the stand which he occupied, and how he had to send a command to the Captains to dismiss their companies which had disobeyed orders repeatedly given to fall in for the review, because there had appeared on the parade ground a man driving a cart with two barrels of ice water.

What a scene this must have been, worthy of the Island of Barataria:—the Colonel bursting with rage, the spectators sizzling with excitement and amusement, the Captains ranting and hoarse with giving orders of which none took notice, the soldiers mobbing the water carrier and his cart, and demanding water; while the Cavalry company, which was well organized and being well drilled, galloped towards the crowd which only separated as the horsemen were almost upon them.

Mr. Charles Morris wrote: "It was with the utmost difficulty, and in obedience to no word of command, that some of us escaped being run over and mangled by the Cavalry." Then he adds: "I laughed, until what with exhaustion from it and the heat, I thought I should die."

The Colonel, disgusted, soon left the field.

It must be remembered, however, that these troops who appeared unmindful of a cocked-hat discipline were soon to become part and parcel of the great army of Northern Virginia, and as the soldiers of the Fifteenth and Fifty-sixth Virginia Regiments of Infantry, and of the Fourth Virginia Regiment of Cavalry, and of the Artillery, that "Long Arm of Lee," were to be known among the bravest and best disciplined soldiers of the Army of Northern Virginia.

The Colonel in the cocked hat and all the military regalia of the Muster Day, and the Captains who "backstraddled" over the young locusts on the Court green not suited for the hardships of the march and the bivouac, were passed by, and the Captain who really drilled the Cavalry troop became a Brigadier, as General Wickham, and the other commands were given to noted drill masters, William Nelson, Lewis Minor Coleman, Frank Terrell, Channing Page, Hilary P. Jones, the Rev. Dabney C. Harrison, Pichegru Woolfolk, Charles William Dabney, and Charles R. Montgomery, whose names are well known in the annals of the Confederacy.

INCIDENTS

Two incidents of unusual interest may be detailed connected with great events which have occurred in Hanover. They relate to the two great protagonists, Lee and Grant, and give an account of what they each were doing in Hanover at a moment of greatest importance to the Confederacy and the Union during the effort to defend Richmond against Grant's army, and his declaration that he would "fight it out on this line if it took all summer."

It was on a June morning of 1864. The Federal troops had been skilfully withdrawn from the upper end of Hanover, where they had crossed the North Anna, and had been quietly moved down through Caroline and King William Counties, and had been put across the Pamunkey at Hanovertown with the intention of breaking into Richmond before Lee, at Hanover Junction (Doswell), could check them. The Union army had crossed without interruption on pontoon bridges, and was marching jauntily along unhindered by Confederate troops.

The Confederate army had marched from the upper end of Hanover with all dispatch to fling itself between Grant and Richmond.

Out of a by-road suddenly dashed an elderly man with a gray beard, riding a gray horse, with two or three young officers who rode hard to keep up with the steady gallop of the gray horse in front. As he reached the highway, the galloping horse was suddenly pulled up, and the rider addressed a general officer in the road in a tone of sharp surprise:

"Why are you stopped here?"

"To meet the enemy in my front," was the answer.

"There is no enemy in your front!" came the words ringing with meaning.

Then the rider turned to a young artilleryman, whose battery was in the road with horses hitched, and said in a tone that filled every saddle in the battery:

"Captain; take your battery, and gallop with all dispath down the road to the Widow Hundley's Corner! 'Tis little more than a mile. There unlimber and fire down the road in your front! Brook no delay. Say to any whom you meet, 'tis General Lee's order! Captain you must hold that point! I shall be near you!" Then he added in a softer tone, which the young officer ever remembered: "Captain; you may have the honor of saving Richmond!"

Along the dusty road from Hanovertown marched the Union army, full of hope and with a confidence it was soon to lose. From the line that has been passing rode into the front gate at "Ingleside," on a sorrel horse, a shaggy-bearded, stocky, blue-eyed, brown haired man, accompanied by several officers in blue uniforms. The man in front, to whom they seemed to pay respect, wore only a blouse with a general's straps on his shoulders.

Addressing the owner of the premises, who came down to meet him, the officer said: "You are Doctor ————. I shall make your yard here my headquarters. You will not be interfered with; but do not leave the premises without my written order." In a few minutes the young officers were sent off, and others rode in and made reports to their chief.

Time hung heavily on the country doctor as he stood

about aimlessly in the yard in which he was now a prisoner.

When the last courier had been dispatched, and there was no other in sight, the officer lighted a fresh cigar and walked towards the corner of the yard. As he passed the owner of the premises, to whom he bowed and offered a cigar, he took out his watch and as if thinking aloud, said: "Unless I hear his guns in five minutes I've got the old fox!"

Then it was the Doctor's time to turn his back and look at his watch. Minutes and seconds never moved so slowly. Thirty seconds passed. Then a minute. Then two minutes. Then two and a half minutes. Then the doctor dropped his watch, and the officer snapped his, and thrust it back into his pocket with an exclamation; for instantly the earth trembled and the heavens seemed filled with noise. Grant and Lee had joined the battle of Second Cold Harbor, and the captain's battery had perhaps saved Richmond, and the bagging of "the old fox," as Grant called Lee that morning in the Ingleside yard.

COUNTY NAMES

The origin of names in Hanover is often lost or only preserved by tradition.

The Indian names have been preserved in Totopotomoi Pamunkey, Chickahominy, Mantico, Powhite, Puccoon, Mahixon, etc; but other names have lost their origin, and are like Little Bo-Peep's sheep. Not but that a few of the older people may know about them, though many familiar names have only tradition to justify their being.

Piping-Tree Ferry, Scotchtown, Rocky Mills, New Castle, all had an origin based on reason in their beginning. Why was Page's Warehouse changed to Hanovertown? As early as 1747 members of the House of Burgesses proposed to remove the Capital from Williamsburg, after the fire that destroyed the buildings, to the Pamunkey River; but the site upon the James at "Shaccoes" eventually prevailed over New Castle, and Hanovertown and the latter place ceased to exist.

Once, however, in the summer of 1864 Hanover became peopled with a great population. It was like Cadmus' city of Thebes after the sowing of the Dragon's teeth, which resulted in the supply of armed men. Grant's soldiers, more than a hundred thousand, crossed the Pamunkey on pontoon bridges here, thinking they had stolen a march on the Confederate Army; but were greatly deceived and found to their sorrow that army was awaiting them on the plains of Cold Harbor, prepared to make of them a "Roman holiday."

Whence came the name Polegreen and Negrofoot? Why was the bridge called Littlepage's? Whence the name Scotchtown or Rug Swamp, or Newfound River, or the Gun-barrel Road? Many of these questions are as much hidden in mystery as the matters relating to "the Cities of the Plain."

The names of the Parishes into which the County was originally divided for political and religious purposes are taken bodily from the parishes in London.

Westminster was St. Peter's Parish. From St. Peter's Parish was cut off St. Paul's, London, and from St. Paul's was cut off St. Martin's in the Field, the latter division being made the year that the Fork Church in St. Martin's Parish, Hanover, was built. (See "The Fork Church" in "Virginia Colonial Churches," edited by Rev. William Meade Clarke.)

So in Hanover St. Paul's was cut off from St. Peter's. Then St. Martin's was cut off from St. Paul's in May, 1726. And in 1742, St. Martin's was divided, and that part west of a line running from the mouth of Gladys Creek on the south side of the river North Anna, a course of South twenty degrees West until it intersected the line of Goochland County, was cut off as Fredericksville. (Hen. Sts.) It is interesting to note that Gladys Creek is in Louisa, and so far has only been found on Bishop Madison's map of Virginia. Its name seems lost, although the line above described is still the boundary between St. Martin's and Trinity Parish, Louisa, which was duly cut off from the eastern end of Fredericksville Parish.

Fredericksville Parish was named after George II's son, Fredrick, the Prince of Wales. He died before his father and his son reigned in his stead as George III.

Of Negrofoot, the tradition is that for an atrocious act of cannibalism, a newly arrived African was drawn and quartered, according to the barbarous law of the time, and parts of the body hung up in various parts of the Colony. As confirmation of the legend, there is a

THE FORK CHURCH.

place in a nearby County called Negro Arm. (See Notes by Charles Morris.)

In 1772, the Virginia House of Burgesses adopted an address to the King protesting against the slave trade, not only because of its inhumanity, but because of its threatening to endanger the very existence of the Colonies, and beseeching him to remove the restraints which forbid their checking so pernicious a commerce. Jefferson in his Notes on Virginia, writes that the proportion of blacks with whites in 1782 was as ten to eleven.

As early as 1773, a citizen of the County of Hanover wrote deploring the situation then existing. From "Scotchtown," which he had acquired in 1771, Patrick Henry wrote, "Hanover, January 18, 1773," acknowledging a book written against the slave trade:

"Is it not amazing, that at a time when the rights of humanity are defined and understood with precision, in a country above all others fond of liberty, we find men professing a religion the most humane * * * adopting a principle as requgnant to humanity as it is inconsistent with the Bible and destructive to liberty?" (W. W. Henry's Life of Patrick Henry, Vol. 1, p. 152.)

Polegreen got its name from a family. The name appears in the Vestry Books of St. Peter's Parish in the account of the meeting held March 31, 1688, and contains the statement that Mr. Geo. Polegreen was of those appointed to cut off Blissland Parish from St. Peter's Parish. The same record shows Mr. Richard Littlepage associated with Mr. Polegreen, and that Mr. John Page was the minister of St. Peter's Parish and for his services was allowed the usual allowance of one thousand pounds of tobacco and cask per month. The minister died soon after, and the vestry book showed that there was due him

November 3, 1688, the amount of 6150 pounds of tobacco. It was ordered at the last named vestry meeting that Mr. John Lightfoot and family be added to ye survey, or of ye highway of ye lower road between the lower church and Black Creek Mill.   (See Vestry Book, St. Peter's Parish.)

When Thomas Nelson Page wrote the "Two Little Confederates," a story of Hanover during the Civil War, he laid the scene at Oakland, which was near Helltown. The publishers said that would never do, so in the "Two Little Confederates," Oakland is located near Hall-town, Jed Hotchkiss' map of the region calls one of the roads "The Helton road."

Bad as it is to lose the history of names, it is worse to be constantly changing them.   Taylor's bridge over the North Anna, near the R. F. and P. Railroad, on the war map used by the Federal army is marked the Chesterfield bridge.   This was natural because the station just north of it on the Railroad was Chesterfield.   It is now Rutherglen, and the name Chesterfield, both as to station and bridge, is lost except upon the war map.   It is now known as Fox's bridge, where a memorial bridge marks "a crisis."

HOMES

The most notable residences in the County are, Studley and Scotchtown, homes of Patrick Henry—the former also the home of Mr. Lyons, and the latter the home of Dorothea Payne (Todd) better known as Dolly Madison; Clay Spring, the birthplace of Henry Clay, destroyed by fire; Taylor's Creek the home of Richard Morris; Hickory Hill the home of General Wickham; Oakland the home of Thomas Nelson Page; and North River the home of Doctor Henry Rose Carter.

Rural Plains, the home of W. R. Shelton is perhaps the oldest residence, long occupied by one family of the same name.

Some Hanover homes are:

Airwell owned by Berkeley and Noland.
Aldingham owned by Dabney, Howard
Alexander's owned by Alexander
Anderson's owned by Anderson
Allen's Creek owned by Doswell, Carter
Annefield owned by Minor, Oliver
Anthony's owned by Anthony
Argonne owned by Bazile
Aspen Grove owned by Duke, Taylor
Auburn Mills owned by Terrell
Albion owned by Vaughan
Baughan's owned by Baughan
Bear Island owned by Gwathmey
Beaver Dam owned by Fontaine, Denoon,
         Regester
Beaver Dam owned by White, Catlin
Beale's owned by Beale
Bell Farm owned by Jenkins

Belmont owned by Taylor
Beazley's owned by Beazley
Betty Mill's owned by Page, Wickham
Big Oak owned by Sacra
Big Rock owned by Bazile
Bleak House owned by Taylor
Blenheim owned by Winston
Bourne's owned by Bourne
Bowles owned by Bowles
Bowe's owned by Bowe
Blunt's owned by Blunt
Bosworth owned by Tyler, Acree
Brackett's owned by Brackett, Stanley
Breeze-Hill owned by Hagan, DeShazo
Breedlove's owned by Breedlove
Broad Neck owned by Page, Va. Manual Labor
        School
Broom Field owned by Berkeley, Lawless Flip-
        po, Campbell
Briarfield owned by Hutchinson, Wickham
Brock Spring owned by Brock, McKenzie
Brown's owned by Brown, Mitchell
Buckeye owned by Pollard, Jones
Bullfield owned by Nelson, Doswell
Bumpass' owned by Bumpass
Burnett owned by Baker
Butler's owned by Butler
Cabin Hill, owned by Carter, Tweatt
Canterbury owned by Meredith
Cason's owned by Cason
Cash Corner owned by Smith, Newton
Cauthorn's owned by Cauthorn
Cedar Grove owned by Newman

Cedar Hill owned by Garnett, Cardozo
Chantilly owned by Coleman, Fleming, Hope
Cherry Dale owned by Morris, Busby, Gilman
 Chilton owned by Nelson, Jackson, Wingfield.
Chisholm's owned by Chisholm, Talley, Wash,
           Page
Churchland owned by Morris, Jones, Stanley
Churchview owned by Morris, Jones
Clazemont owned by Morris, Jones
Cooke's owned by Cooke, Richeson
Cool Springs owned by Oliver Cridlin
Coatesville owned by Coates, Beazley
Cocke's owned by Cocke
Clifton owned by Alexander
Clover Lea owned by Bassett, Haw, West
Colley Swamp owned by Fontaine, Cooke
Cool Water owned by Price, Vandenburg, Grubb,
           Oliver
Cottage owned by Carlton
Cottage owned by Oliver
Crewsville owned by Crew, Terrell
Courtland owned by Winston
Craney Island owned by Meredith, Lumpkins
           Thomas
Cross' owned by Cross
Crow's owned by Crow
Crump's Neck owned by Haw
Dalton owned by Cardwell, Dabney
Darracott's owned by Darracott, Vaughan, Har-
           rison
Davenport's owned by Davenport,
Dewberry owned by Cooke, White, Dixon
Diamond Hill owned by Williams, Norment

Ditchley owned by Tomlin, Skidmore
Dogwood Lodge owned by Cooke
Dry Bridge owned by Baker
Dundee owned by Price, Haw
Dungarvon owned by Sydnor, Via
Dulce Domo owned by Bassett
Eastview owned by Terrell Pearsall
Eastview owned by Turner
Eastwood owned by Jones, Evans
Edgewood owned by Berkeley, Minor, Noland
Eddleton's owned by Eddleton
Ellington owned by Fox, Richards
Elmington owned by Anderson, Luck, Saunders
Elmwood owned by Cross, Mallory
Elon owned by Anderson, Spencer
Emmett owned by Terrell
Fairfield owned by Nelson, Lowry, Vaughan,
Parrish
Fairfield owned by Overton, Gaines.
Fairview owned by Harris
Farmer's owned by Farmer
Forest Hill owned by Duke, Stringfellow, Lowry
Forest Lawn owned by Vaughan
Farmington owned by Bassett, Macon
Fountain Inn owned by Ball, Cullen
French Hay owned by Wooldridge, Perrin
Furlong owned by Converse
Garland Hill owned by Carter
Gilman's owned by Gilman
Glazebrook's owned by Glazebrook
Glencairn owned by Shepherd, Campbell
The Glimpse owned by Boyd, Jones
Goodall's owned by Goodall, Nash

Gould Hill owned by Nelson, Brockenbrough,
Newton, Lee
Goshen owned by Nelson, Fulcher, Martin, Page
Gray's owned by Gray
Greenwood owned by Taylor
Greenwood owned by Allen, Anderson
Greenbay owned by Jones
 Greenland owned by Howard, Davis
Greenfields owned by Green
The Grove owned by Pendleton, Wickham
Gum Spring owned by Noble, Wickham
Green's owned by Green
 Greenway owned by Pollard, Vial
Hammond's owned by Hammond
Hancock's owned by Hancock
Hanovertown owned by Page
Hanover Academy owned by Coleman, Jones
Hardin's owned by Hardin
Harris' owned by Harris
Hardbargain owned by Holloway
Hawbuck˙ owned by Ellett, Duke, Lowry
Haw's Shop owned by Haw
Hatch's owned by Hatch
Hewlett owned by Hewlett, Maddox, Powers,
Duke
Hickory Bottom owned by Brown, Taylor,
Wickham, Williamson
Hickory Hill owned by Wickham
Hickory Hill owned by Terrell, Hall
Higginson's owned by Higginson, Jacobs
Hill Fork owned by Davidson, Sledd, Haw
Hilly Farm owned by Jones.
Hilly Home owned by Gilman
Holladay's owned by Holladay, Wood

Hollowing Creek owned by Hall, Richardson
Hollingsworth's owned by Hollingsworth
Holly Hill owned by Brown
Horne's owned by Horne
Horse Shoe owned by Braxton, Bassett, Smith
Horse Shoe owned by James, Bumpass
Horse Shoe owned by Terrell, Jackson
Horse Shoe owned by Lumpkin, Gilman
Howard's Neck owned by Sydnor
Humanity Hall owned by Nelson, Butler
Hundley owned by Hundley
Hybla owned by Redd
Ingleside owned by Braxton, Tomlin, Macon,
                    Dillard, Dumbell
Island Ford owned by Anderson, Minor
Ivy Bank owned by Ellett
James' owned by James
Johnson's owned by Johnson
Janeway owned by Cooke, Hunter
Jones Cross Rds. owned by Jones, Beazley,
                    Smith
Jones' owned by Jones
King's owned by Cross, Gilman
Kilby owned by Kilby
Krishnaghur owned by Berkeley, Pollard
Langford's owned by Langford, Shelton
Lancaster's owned by Lancaster
Lakeview owned by Luck
Laurel Branch owned by Montgomery
Laurel Spring owned by Truehart, Ellerson
Laurel Grove owned by Palmer, Long
Lessland owned by Hunter, Remsen, Taylor
Leftwich's owned by Leftwich

Liberty Hall owned by Truehart, Starke, Sledd
Little Eagle owned by Perkins
Locust Green owned by Richardson
Littlepage's owned by Littlepage, Thornton,
       Hunt, Lewis
Lloyd's owned by Lloyd
Locust Grove owned by Vaughan
Locust Grove owned by Thompson
Locust Level owned by Robinson, Chisholm
Locust Row owned by Terrell, Bell
Locust Grove owned by Nuckols
Logton owned by Doswell, Terry
Lone Pine owned by Dodge, Staples
Lowry's owned by Lowry
La Madelaine owned by Fox
Mantico owned by Terrell, Johnson
Martin's owned by Martin
Maple Grove owned by Noel
Maple Wood owned by Carroll, Bigger, Ham-
    mond
Mannheim owned by Winston, Cox
Mayfield owned by Adkisson, Sydnor, Mosby
Meadow Farm owned by Sydnor
The Meadow owned by Talley, Wickham
Mahixon owned by Page, Redd
Mechumps owned by Hamilton
Mechump's Ridge owned by Luck
Medley Grove owned by Priddy
Mechanicsville owned by Lumpkin, Strain
Marlbourne owned by Ruffin
Melrose owned by Ellett, Davis
Merry Oaks owned by Lipscomb, Perrin, Jenkins
Mica Mine owned by Barr, Henry, Saunders

Mineral Spring owned by Baker
Mineral Spring owned by Hall, Redd
Mont Air owned by Nelson, Taylor, Page
Mount Airy owned by Gilman, Lumpkin
  Montpelier owned by Morris, Jones, Isbell
Mount Pleasant owned by Sutton, Cady
Mount Pleasant owned by Terrell
Mon Tout owned by Berkeley, Harris
Montevideo owned by Ellett, Harris
Moreland owned by Coleman, Hunter
Nelson's owned by Nelson
Negrofoot owned by Korb, Mills, Thompson
Netherland's owned by Clements
Noel owned by Landrum
Newcastle owned by Braxton, Broaddus, Alex-
                 ander
North River owned by Price, Carter
Norment's owned by Norment
Nuckol's owned by Nuckols
Nutshell owned by Woodson, Woolfolk
Oak Grove owned by Haw
Oak Grove owned by Ellett
Oak Level owned by Terrell
The Oaks owned by Cardwell
Oakley Hill owned by Sydnor
Oakland owned by Nelson, Page
Oak Lawn owned by Bigger, Crawford, Cobb
Old Ark owned by Haw
Old Glebe owned by Nelson, Lowry
Offley owned by Nelson, Hicks, Noland, Cooke
Oak Ridge owned by Wingfield
Pagerie La owned by Page
Passadena owned by Vaughan, Haley

Parrish's owned by Parrish
Paradise owned by Huffman
Peake's owned by Peake, Dyson
Perkins owned by Perkins
Phillips' owned by Phillips
Pigeon Hill owned by Fontaine, Johnson, Cooke
Pinecote owned by F. L. Page, Visiting Nurse
           Association
Plain Dealing owned by Thomas, Parkinson,
           Woolfolk, Dyson
Plain View owned by Hendrick, Lowry
Pleasant Level owned by Anderson, Ladd, Clarke
Plum Orchard owned by Austin, Puller
Point Lookout owned by Thacker
Prospect Hill owned by Cardwell
Pohite owned by Gaines
Polegreen owned by Polegreen
Pollard's owned by Pollard
Poplar Spring owned by Glazebrook, Gilman
Poverty Hill owned by Anderson
Puccoon owned by Curtis
Raleigh owned by Waldrop
Ratcliffe owned by Taylor, Day
Red Hill owned by Hendrick
Retreat owned by Waddill
Retirement owned by Tyler, Bazile
Riverside owned by Hall, Fontaine, Sharp
           Stanley
Rice's owned by Rice
Rockett's owned by Price, Oliver
Rockcastle owned by Fontaine, Gilman, Carter
Rocky Mills owned by Syme, Wickham, Nash,
           Stanley, Nolting
Rose Hall owned by Noel

Rose Hill owned by Vaughan, Carter
Rose Level owned by Moody
Rowzie's owned by Rowzie
Rug Swamp owned by Page, Davis, Chisholm, Waldrop, Bartlett
Rural Plains owned by Shelton
Rutledge owned by Timberlake
Santee owned by Macon
Scotchtown owned by Henry, Cary, Dandridge, Shepherd, Taylor
Selwyn owned by Macon, Hogan, Curtis
Shelton's owned by Shelton
Shady Grove owned by Christian
Shelburn's owned by Shelburn, Baughan
Shrubbery Hill owned by Crenshaw, Jones, Boys 'Home
Signal Hill owned by Winston, Vaughan
Slash Cottage owned by Thompson
Sligo owned by Redd
Smith's owned by Baughan, Smith
Snead Swamp owned by Wickham
South Wales owned by Littlepage, Carter. Winston, Skilman, Carter
Souther's owned by McChesney
Springfield owned by Christian, Lumpkin
Springfield owned by Nelson, Fulcher, Wilkie
Springfield owned by Winn
Spring Garden owned by Roane, Meredith
Summerhill owned by Newton, Christian
Stanley's owned by Braxton, Webb
Stone's owned by Stone
Stanley's owned by Stanley, Wickham

Swift's owned by Swift

Studley owned by Syme, Henry, Lyons, Norment, Greenlee

Talley's owned by Talley

Tarboro owned by Tyler, Curtis

Tan Yard owned by Thompson, Taylor

Tan Yard owned by Moody, Goodman

Taylorsville owned by Taylor

Taylor's Creek owned by Morris

Teddington owned by Tomlin

Telcourt owned by Wightman, Peck

Terrell's owned by Terrell

Thompson's owned by Thompson

Tignor's owned by Tignor

Traveller's Rest owned by Moody

The Triangle owned by Barret

Turkey Hill owned by Perkins, Bowles

Tucker's owned by Tucker

Totomoi owned by Tinsley, Jones

Turner's owned by Turner

Tyler's owned by Tyler

Vass' owned by Vass

Vadens owned by Vaden, Brown, Shelton

Vaughan's owned by Vaughan

Verdon owned by Anderson

Walton's owned by Walton, Cox

Walnut Well owned by Harris

Walnut Lane owned by Austin, Sydnor, Tener

Walnut Shade owned by Stuart, Campbell

Watkins' owned by Watkins

Walton's owned by Walton, Nuckols, Vaughan

Watt's owned by Watt

White's owned by White

White Hall owned by Cowell
White House owned by Berkeley, Wallenger
Welcome Home owned by Moody
Westfield owned by Fontaine, Spicer
  Westview owned by Turner
Westview owned by Darracott
  Westwood owned by Parsley
West's owned by West
Wharton's owned by Johnson
Williamsville owned by Pollard
White Oak owned by White, Gilman
Wilton owned by Winston
Willow-brook owned by Taylor
Wiltshire owned by Wiltshire
Willis' owned by Willis
Wingfield owned by Nelson, Hart
Woodbury owned by Peatross, Peace
Woodfin's owned by Woodfin
Woolfolk's owned by Woolfolk
Woodgrove owned by Winston, Cooke, Quarles
Woodland owned by Winston, Banks
Woodlawn owned by Saunders, Jones, Sharp
Wormeley's owned by Wormeley
Wright's owned by Wright

In writing of the people of Hanover and their life, one is pleased to find them at every period worthy of their lineage, and that they have at all times been true to form, and displayed the qualities of loyal Virginians, and patriotic Americans.

THE END

INDEX